Alighiero e Boetti

Whitechapel Art Gallery

Contents

Foreword

One of the leading artists associated with Arte Povera, Alighiero Boetti remains the least known and certainly the least exhibited in this country. Yet today, looking back at thirty years of richly inventive activity, he emerges as a quiet master of contemporary art. His ability to transform the commonplace into the profound, to treat the complex with extreme simplicity and humour, captivates, amuses, even seduces.

Boetti never adhered to any particular movement or tendency, seemed to shun any prescriptive or generalising force. There is both chance and a measure of elaborate design in the work of this Italian artist, who assimilated the culture of New York and Afghanistan as easily as that of Rome. Capable of making art from a torn scrap of paper, or inspired by a sunny day in Turin, he also aspired to capture the world, to re-write language or to immerse us in a new philosophy of numbers.

Alighiero Boetti was an artist the Whitechapel had hoped for many years to show. The exhibition that Judith Nesbitt proposed last August was one that would concentrate on key periods and indeed key works, distributed in the open, light-filled spaces of the Whitechapel. We are delighted to be able to mount the exhibition to coincide with the Italian Festival, taking place this autumn. The involvement of the Archivio Alighiero Boetti has been essential in guiding us, and we are deeply indebted to Caterina Raganelli Boetti, and to Agata and Matteo Boetti for their support, as well as to the Archivio for agreeing to collaborate on the exhibition. The research has benefited extensively from existing work undertaken in preparation for the forthcoming catalogue raisonné, supervised by Germano Celant, while Antonella Soldaini, who acted as co-curator with Judith Nesbitt, has written a considered text which puts Boetti's practice within its art historical perspective. We are delighted that Shirazeh Houshiary, Sol LeWitt, Mario Codognato and Giovan Battista Salerno agreed to share their insights and personal knowledge of Boetti and his work. Diletta Borromeo added a detailed account of the artist's oeuvre.

The organisation of the exhibition, largely undertaken by Andrea Tarsia, curator at the Whitechapel, with other colleagues at the gallery, depended upon many with personal histories linked to Boetti and to Italian art; amongst those we would like to thank are Annemarie Sauzeau Boetti, and Gianfranco Benedetti, Baron Giorgio Franchetti, Eric Franck, Ingvild Goetz, Rolf Lauter, Nicholas Ward-Jackson, Henry Meyric Hughes, Peter Marsin and Massimo Minini. We would like to express our special gratitude to those, listed elsewhere in these pages, who made works available from their collections. It is a mark of their commitment to the work of Boetti that they responded so readily to our requests. Lastly, certainly not least, we are indebted to Kate Stephens, for her design of this publication, and to Ben Craze and Pale Green Press.

Catherine Lampert
Director

Alighiero e Boetti

Alighiero Boetti has been variously described as an abstract artist and as a figurative artist, conceptual and minimal, a performer, a philosopher, a practising musician, an amateur mathematician. It is perhaps because of this, because of his magical ability to be many people rather than one (Alighiero *and* Boetti), that younger artists today – especially in Italy – see him as a true *maître penseur*. Resisting the temptation to dramatise the artist's life and, by extension, his work, this text concentrates on the known facts of Boetti's career, without providing a single, unifying reading of his practice and personality.

Boetti had no formal art training, but became interested in contemporary art through a series of exhibitions that he visited in Turin (his home city) and on regular visits to France, in the period between 1960 and 1965. He admired Italian artists such as Giorgio Morandi, Giacomo Balla, Lucio Fontana, but also the work of Arshile Gorky, Mark Rothko, Wols, Henri Michaux, Cy Twombly, Paul Klee, Nicolas De Staël and Jean Dubuffet. From the outset, Boetti was also drawn to artistic production outside Europe. "…[In Paris] I saw my first exhibition of Japanese monks and their Zen paintings – the circle drawn in one gesture with a big brush dipped in black ink…Then another event marked my view of the world. I understood only later that it was the exhibition that André Malraux – at the time minister of Cultural Affairs - held at the Fondation Maeght in Vence, France, which brought together all the beautiful things he had encountered in his travels around the world. For me it was my first global vision of art. I remember a white marble Babylonian sculpture with a full beard and eyes of lapis lazuli, then a Khmer sculpture of grey granite, and the perfect life-size Egyptian scribe of wood…For me it was a concentration of completely unknown worlds, new images, new desires, new ideas, new cultures…"[1] Boetti's first works, completed during the same period, include landscapes in oil loosely inspired by De Staël, and a series of Indian ink drawings on paper (fig. 67). Depicting industrial objects such as binoculars, microphones and cine cameras, the tightly controlled execution of these early drawings – "drawn", he said, "as only an industrial draughtsman can draw"[2] - belies their lingering sense of metaphysical disquiet.

Around 1966, Boetti moved into his first studio in Turin and began to associate with a number of local artists, including Gianni Piacentino, Piero Gilardi and Michelangelo Pistoletto. Their practice at the time responded to aspects of the American avant-garde, which in those years was gaining increasing recognition across Europe. That same year the three artists participated in *Arte Abitabile* [Habitable Art] at Galleria Gian Enzo Sperone in Turin, presenting works which sought to create a more direct contact with everyday reality by referencing commonplace objects - an approach exemplified by Pistoletto's *Oggetti in meno* [Minus Objects]. 1966 was also a year of intense productivity for Boetti, who made a series of works exhibited in January 1967 in his first solo exhibition, at Galleria Christian Stein in Turin. Stein, Sperone and Galleria L'Attico in Rome (run by Fabio Sargentini) were among the first to showcase the work of a new generation of Italian artists who soon would be grouped together under the 'Arte Povera' banner.

Boetti's first solo exhibition at Galleria Stein (fig. 2) included seminal early works such as *Lampada annuale* [Yearly Lamp] (fig. 22), *Ping Pong* (fig. 23), *Mimetico* [Camouflage] (fig. 35), *Rotolo di cartone ondulato* [Roll of Corrugated Fiberboard][3], *Catasta* [Stack], *Sedia* [Chair], *Scala* [Ladder] (fig. 21), *Mancorrente metri 2* [Hand Rail 2 Metres] (fig. 68), *Tubi* [Tubes] and *Zig Zag* (fig. 28). Asked to discuss these works the artist stated - in keeping with the cultural climate of the period - that "…if *Lampada annuale* is a fundamentally literary work… with all its cultural and literary referents, its need for a justification, for a logical continuation etc.; then in the latest works – *Catasta*, *Tubi*, *Rotolo di cartone ondulato*, *Tessuto 8.50* [Fabric 8.50][4] – I can only say that [they are] a stack, a roll of cardboard pushed upwards from the inside, a bundle of tubes etc. All analytical superstructures have collapsed; the only focus is on the elementary and non-signifying action."[5] The statement clearly reveals a need to erase all ideological structures, perceived as obstacles to a direct contact with real life and events. Significantly, the artist never referred to his works as 'sculptures' during this period, but rather as 'objects' that focused exclusively on the type of material used. The invitation to the exhibition at Galleria Stein reflected this approach. Samples of the ten materials used in making the works on show were attached to the card, their names listed underneath: "camouflage fabric, cork letter, asbestos lumber, copper, plywood, Perspex,

fig.1
Alighiero Boetti,
1970

PVC tube, wire netting, aluminium, electric cable" (fig. 3). In other works produced in 1966, also exhibited at Stein, the same preoccupation with a reduction of meaning is played out with words rather than materials. In *Stiff Upper Lip* (fig. 34), *The Thin Thumb* (fig. 33), *Clino* and *Frou Frou* each work's meaning is tautologically inscribed within the work itself and reduced to a single, playful, statement that refers to common phrases and images.

The exhibition at Galleria Stein gave Boetti almost instant access to a thriving and diverse cultural network. "…from complete isolation, I suddenly found myself in a certain situation…where for the first time I saw critics, including Celant, and artists, including Zorio, amongst the various people who attended the show…Suddenly I found myself in this world…Palazzoli arrived, Trini, Henry Martin…then La Bertesca [Gallery] became interested, Pistoletto came up to me, and things took off from there…"[6] That same summer he started on *12 forme dal 10 giugno 1967* [12 Shapes from 10 June 1967], completed in 1971, consisting of twelve copper sheets, each etched with the shape of a political territory then in a state of war (fig. 41). Here, for the first time, the artist explored themes that he would return to in subsequent works: an interest in political and current affairs, mapping, the idea of tracing and that of creating a work which develops over a period of years.

In September 1967 Germano Celant curated a definitive exhibition entitled *Arte povera e Im spazio* at Galleria La Bertesca in Genoa. The Arte Povera section included, besides Boetti, Luciano Fabro, Emilio Prini, Jannis Kounellis, Giulio Paolini and Pino Pascali. Inspired by Jerzy Grotowski's 'Poor Theatre', Celant first coined the term 'Arte Povera' on this occasion, elucidating the principles implicit in the work so named: "…Thus, in the visual arts, visual and plastic reality are seen as they happen and as they are. They are reduced to their linguistic artifices. Visual *complicatio*, unconnected with the essence of the object, is done away with. Language is acknowledged and reduced to a purely visual element, divested of historical and narrative superstructures. The empirical quality of artistic enquiry, rather than its speculative aspect, is exalted. The hard facts and the physical presence of an object, or the behaviour of a subject, is emphasised…"[7] For the exhibition Boetti exhibited *Catasta*, made of asbestos lumber tubes that, when stacked one above the other, form a parallelepipedal structure: "…When I made *Catasta* with asbestos lumber tubes, I had gone to a building yard. I couldn't believe my eyes when I saw the amazing things to be found there! There really was everything, from firebricks – which are very beautiful – to fiberglass, polystyrene, everything just lying there…"[8]

Boetti's second solo exhibition took place later that year at Galleria La Bertesca, and was accompanied by his first catalogue. This featured essays by Celant, 'Per i ciechi tutto è improvviso' [Everything is sudden for the blind], Tommaso Trini, 'Blocchi che sbloccano' [Blocks that Unblock], and an untitled essay by Henry Martin - three critics who were particularly alive to the artistic events of the period. The works on show, such as *Tavelle* [Tiles] (fig. 24), *Eternit 9* [Asbesto Lumber 9] (fig. 69) *Cemento 360* [Cement 360] and *Ferro legno 8* [Iron Wood 8], furthered his investigation into the value of industrial materials and were formally even more rigorous than those included in his first solo exhibition. As with earlier works, he selected the materials precisely because they lacked any symbolic or cultural referent. In his catalogue essay, Celant wrote: "…Emptied of any iconography or specificity, the material only emphasises composition, formation, never the effect. There are no expressive nuances or overtones, there is no relationship of empathy. These compositions belong to everyday observations, they do not create a dialogue with the viewer, providing him with a cultural gap to fill; they are 'figures' that have been constructed, cut out and erected, presented with exactitude. They are the way they are…"[9]

Towards the end of 1967, Boetti completed one of the most enigmatic and playful works of his early career. Entitled *Manifesto*, it listed the names of fifteen Italian artists, besides his own, all of them friends of Boetti's at the time and belonging to the same circle of emerging younger artists (fig. 30). A different combination of eight symbols was placed next to each name, their coded meaning still unknown to us. According to the artist the key to these symbols was deposited with a Notary, who was authorised to release it to anyone who paid the appropriate fee.[10] However, despite

fig.2
Galleria Christian Stein, Turin,
January 1967

fig.3*
Invitation card for the exhibition at
Galleria Christian Stein, Turin,
January 1967

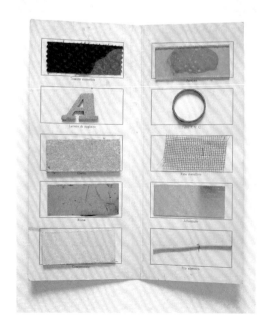

extensive research undertaken to date, no proof has yet been found that he did deposit the 'key' to *Manifesto* in this way.[11]

The Venice Biennale of 1968 took place in a climate of widespread dissent, which culminated with police intervention and with several artists deciding to close off the rooms allocated to them (at the end of the preceding year Celant had published an article eloquently titled 'Arte Povera. Notes For A Guerrilla War').[12] 1968 was also the year in which the key Arte Povera exhibitions took place. These consecrated it as a movement, one capable of mediating and positioning itself in relation to the arrival on the European scene of American artists belonging to minimal, conceptual and land art. While alert to the disquiet that typified the moment, Boetti also remained focused on the more personal developments of his own artistic practice: "… I aimed to think about my own things, which absorbed me entirely. I lived all these political events in a very detached manner…"[13]

In February 1968, Boetti had his second solo exhibition at Galleria Christian Stein. It presented several new works, characterised by a playful irony that opened up new linguistic possibilities: *Panettone*, *Legnetti colorati* [Small Coloured Sticks] (fig. 27), *Palla corda* [Ball Rope] and *Bilancia* [Weighing Scale]. Also included were two sections of corrugated fiberboard, one of which bore the inscription BOETTI (printed across the top in block capitals), while on the other the same word appeared written in reverse: ITTEOB. This was one of the first instances in which the artist made play of his name and where reversed inscriptions appear.[14] That same month he was invited by Celant to participate in *Arte Povera*, held at Galleria de' Foscherari in Bologna. Boetti made a second poster specifically for the exhibition which, like the first, also presented a map – although this time quite literally – of the artistic scene of the period. Titled *Città di Torino* [City of Turin], the work consisted in a drawn map of his home city on which the artist indicated the addresses of friends who were also participating to the show. In April, Galleria De Nieubourg in Milan organised a solo exhibition titled *Shaman Showman*, for which Boetti made a third poster (with the same title), that was fly-posted on walls across the city. On this occasion, the artist focused on his own self-image as a play on artistic identity: the poster bore an image from Eliphas Lévi's *Histoire de la Magie*, published in 1860, which the artist modified slightly by replacing the face of one of the two figures with his own (fig. 7). His use of this image indicates the artist's thorough knowledge of the worlds of alchemy and the Cabala, as well as the breadth of his interests at that time. It is at the very least surprising that, in a period of politicised activity, Boetti should choose to post a manifesto that alludes to hermetic knowledge and to the notion of the artist as a magician. The text accompanying the image in Lévi's book, though somewhat obscure, is nonetheless significant when read in relation to the Boetti's interests: "…the thirty-two absolute meanings of words, of numbers and letters, should be applied; each letter reproduces a number, an idea and a shape, so that mathematicians should apply themselves to ideas and shapes as rigorously as they do to numbers, in accordance with an exact proposition and a perfect equivalence."[15] The artist's conception of art as an almost secret activity, similar in its methods of research to that of esoteric sciences, is evident in a work produced by another artist, SALVO, who had become a close friend of Boetti's in the early years of their career. Until the early 70s both shared similar interests, including a preoccupation with the philosophy of linguistics, and with the idea of maps. In SALVO's *Salvo e Boetti come I Sette Savi che scrutano il moto degli astri* [Salvo and Boetti As the Seven Sages Scrutinising the Movement of the Stars], 1969, both artists appear as ancient wise men busy exploring the mysteries of the cosmos (fig. 8).

For the exhibition in Milan, Boetti created an imaginary location - a garden of sorts - in which the works were not isolated from each other but became an integral part of the whole (fig. 4). He filled the gallery with pebbles, as though the bed of a small rivulet, and through it created a pathway. Amongst the works he presented were a series of *Colonne* [Columns], made by stacking paper doilies (fig. 4); a series of Plexiglas cubes filled with a variety of materials (fig. 5); an ensemble of small coloured sticks (*Legnetti Colorati*) which, placed amongst the

fig.4
Galleria De Nieubourg, Milan,
23 April 1968

fig.5*
Senza titolo
[Untitled]
ca.1967
Plexiglas, wood, polystyrene, iron,
plastic, Kapok, chipboard, cork
50 x 60 x 60 cm
Private collection, London

stones, formed a sort of flower bed (fig. 27);[16] and *Autoritratto in negativo* [Negative self-portrait], a natural stone that had been hollowed out and moulded on the artist. During this period, Boetti was particularly interested in making works that could be placed in natural surroundings; he made seven versions of *Autoritratto…*, placing them in a variety of locations such as a riverbed, a mountaintop and a park.[17]

    Gemelli [Twins], 1968, a photograph in postcard form, further elucidates the artist's preoccupation with themes of division, the double and dualities, already present in *Shaman Showman* and in early works such as *Ping Pong*. Using photomontage, Boetti depicts himself holding hands with another similar, but not identical self (fig. 6). Giovan Battista Salerno, a critic who remained one of his closest friends, wrote the following about *Gemelli*: "It would be wonderful if there were two worlds - the one entirely conscious, the other entirely subconscious - that held hands with each other without ever becoming blurred, instead of somehow finding themselves both monstrously contained within the vessel that is the anguished subject".[18] One of the first examples of mail art – the postcard was sent to friends and associates - *Gemelli* is a seminal work, one that re-elaborated concepts of identity and which was further developed in 1972, when the artist made the significant gesture of signing his works as Alighiero 'e' [and] Boetti. This nomenclature, which Boetti maintained for the rest of his life, reinforced the idea of the self as being double: "Alighiero is the more infantile side, more external, which dominates familiar things. Alighiero is the way in which those who know me call and name me. Boetti is more abstract, precisely because a surname is a category. While a name is unique, a surname is already a category, a means of classification…".[19]

    RA3 Arte Povera + Azioni Povere, held in October 1968 at the Antichi Arsenali della Repubblica in Amalfi, represented a culminating moment in the collective activity of Arte Povera artists. It was the first exhibition to show international artists within the context of the Italian art movement and, staged in an old naval shipyard, also featured a series of performances held throughout the city as well as on its neighbouring beach. Curated by Celant, it included Boetti, Giovanni Anselmo, Riccardo Camoni, Ger Van Elk, Paolo Icaro, Jannis Kounellis, Pietro Lista, Richard Long, Gino Marotta, Plinio Martelli, Marisa Merz, Mario Merz, Giulio Paolini, Pino Pascali, Gianni Piacentino, Michelangelo Pistoletto, Annemarie Sauzeau (Boetti's first wife), Gilberto Zorio and the 'Guitti dello Zoo' (Ableo, Colnaghi, Martin, Maria Pioppi and Pistoletto). Boetti presented a group of objects ("…I exhibited a group of things…")[20] which aimed to bring the public into contact with the artist's 'laboratory space', rather than with a finished work (fig. 9). Talking about these works and their presentation, he said: "These are not art objects, but suggested conceptual approaches to reality, to life, because we have all been conditioned, alienated…for example, I showed a small box filled with perfume, and nobody but children dared to come over and smell it."[21]

After the exhibition in Amalfi, Boetti felt the need to distance himself from what had occurred until then. From a period of tremendous creative ebullience, in which the need to communicate had prevailed, his attention moved inwards, towards thought, its processes, its qualities of analysis and research: "…as for me, until '68, which ended with the exhibition in Amalfi, I followed the direction of those well-known exhibitions…then I started to doubt that direction. There had been too much focus on materials. In the end they had almost become more important than everything else. It had become like a grocery store. Therefore, yes, I remember that in the spring of '69 I left the studio I had in Turin, which had become a warehouse for materials, full of asbestos lumber, cement, stones. I left everything exactly as it was and started again from scratch, with a pencil and a sheet of paper. I took a sheet of squared paper and made a picture, *Cimento dell'armonia e dell'invenzione* [Contest Between Harmony and Invention]. It consisted of re-tracing each square. This is what starting again meant for me."[22] In this work (fig. 13) the artist limited his intervention to retracing alone, 'forcing' himself to follow a prescribed path while still succeeding in leaving a personal trace (if an almost invisible one): "…the experience of the small squares was one that I can't convey, but an incredible one, because I found myself in front of a completely new space, and with this support, or the idea of retracing…it gave me tremendous freedom…All manner of things happened in those squares, I wrote some terrible or beautiful things, secret things which were then filled in because the only rule was to fill in, without any constraints of time or of reason, especially the first times…"[23]

fig.6*
Gemelli
[Twins]
1968
photograph and mixed media on paper
postcard
13.5 x 9.5 cm
An enlarged photograph, measuring
100 x 70 cm, has been produced for this
exhibition.

fig.7
Shaman Showman
1968
offset print
100 x 70 cm

fig.8
Salvo e Boetti come i Sette Savi che scrutano il moto degli astri
by SALVO
[Salvo and Boetti As the Seven Sages
Scrutinising the Movement of the Stars]
1969
photoprint and drawing on canvas
180 x 120 cm

In 1969 Harald Szeeman invited Boetti to participate in *Live in Your Head. When Attitudes Become Form: Works, Concepts, Processes, Situations, Information*, held at the Kunsthalle Bern. The exhibition was one of the first to bring conceptual, land and Arte Povera artists together in a museum space, and explored alternative exhibiting models often dictated by the works themselves. Boetti shared a space with Bruce Nauman and presented new works, among them *La Luna* [The Moon], 1969 and *Io prendo il sole a Torino il 24-2-69* [Me sunbathing in Turin on 24-2-69] (fig. 26). This last work was also exhibited in May as part of his solo exhibition at Galleria Gian Enzo Sperone,[24] together with *Una Vetrata* [A Window][25] (fig. 20) - and *Ritratto di Walter De Maria* [Portrait of Walter De Maria]. These three works are formally very diverse and one - *Ritratto di Walter De Maria* (fig. 77) - has since been lost. The use of cement in *Io che prendo il sole...* evokes earlier works, although here the hardness of the material is offset by the artist's lyrical treatment of subject matter. Based on his own body, the figure is composed of individual pieces of cement that bear the imprint of his hand, a cabbage butterfly placed at chest height on one of the cement blocks. *Vetrata*, on the other hand, represented a shift towards the thought processes involved in creating a work and re-proposed, this time on a large scale, the concepts of the grid and of 'fullness' and 'emptiness' already present in *Cimento dell'armonia...*

Setting out to delve into scientific axioms and to test the reliability of supposedly 'scientific' information, in 1970 Boetti started to conceive the idea of classifying the longest rivers in the world. Working with Annemarie Sauzeau, who undertook all the related research and documentation, they contacted geographic societies and universities, collecting data from encyclopaedias and specialist studies until, in 1977, the work was completed with the publication of *Classificazione dei mille fiumi più lunghi del mondo* [Classifying the Thousand Longest Rivers of the World] (fig. 16). This research, which began with a straight forward survey, led them to conclude that "...both the partial information existing on the rivers, the linguistic problems tied in with their identities and the intangible nature of water, mean that this classification – as with all preceding or subsequent ones – will always be provisional and illusory."[26] Besides the publication, the research resulted in two large tapestries, made between 1976 and 1982, which listed the rivers in descending order (starting with the longest) and were produced in a green (fig. 87) and a white version.

In 1969 Boetti had begun a complex postal work, *Dossier Postale* [Postal Dossier], through which he metaphorically enabled 25 people (chosen amongst friends, relatives, artists, critics and gallerists) to 'travel' on an imaginary postal journey (fig. 78).[27] From 1970 this type of production increased in regularity – a practice developed in the same period by artists such as On Kawara and Douglas Huebler.[28] *Untitled*, 1970, consisted of six letters sent to Galleria Sperone, on which the artist arranged 50, 70 and 80 Lira stamps in all possible sequential combinations (in this case six). The artist soon developed his analysis of combinational possibilities into works of considerable scale and complexity, such as *Senza numero I-VI* [Un-numbered I-VI], 1972 (which consists of 720 envelopes, see fig. 46); or with considerable poetic force, such as *Untitled*, 1979, dedicated to his mother (fig. 45). Between 1969 and 1970 Boetti took part in several exhibitions (*Op Losse Schroeven* and *Processi di Pensiero Visualizzati*) which emphasised artistic thought processes rather than the art object. Sol LeWitt's 'Paragraphs on Conceptual Art', published in 1967, was particularly important to Boetti. LeWitt wrote: "...If the artist carries through his idea and makes it into visible form, then all the steps in the process are of importance. The idea itself, even if not made visual, is as much a work of art as any finished product. All intervening steps – scribbles, sketches, drawings, failed works, models, studies, thoughts, conversations – are of interest. Those that show the thought process of the artist are sometimes more interesting than the final product..."[29]

During *Aktionsraum 1*, held in Munich in 1970, Boetti carried out a rare series of performances: he held a conference in Esperanto; cut a piece of paper in half and then in half again, and so on - a procedure he later termed *Raddoppiare dimezzando* [Doubling by Halving] (fig. 37); measured his height in relation to that of a tree and, finally, wrote a phrase across a wall using both hands. The

fig.9
Antichi Arsenali della Repubblica,
Amalfi,
October 1968

fig.10
**Oggi è venerdì ventisette marzo
millenovecentosettanta ore...**
[Today is Friday Twenty Seventh May
Nineteenseventy at...]
1970
simultaneous writing with both hands on
wall
dimensions variable

phrase - 'punto, puntino, zero, goccia, germe' [dot, small dot, zero, drop, seed] – was taken from Normann O. Brown's *Love's Body*, published in 1966. The text's innovative approach to the study of 'reality', examined through the filters of psychoanalysis, anthropology and oriental philosophy, greatly influenced the artist in his thinking.[30] In Munich, he wrote Brown's phrase with both hands simultaneously, starting from the centre and proceeding in opposite directions. On the right hand side, the phrase developed normally, but on the other (from the centre towards the left) it became completely illegible (see for example figs.10 and 82). For the artist, this process transformed writing into drawing ("...to write with one's left hand is to draw..."),[31] in that each individual letter was written backwards, as though an exercise in mirror writing.

The early seventies marked a turning point for Boetti, and for the avant-garde in general, as the utopia and optimism which had charged the previous decade turned to a more critical sense of malaise. After an intense series of large group exhibitions, Arte Povera artists turned to more individual concerns. On March 15th 1971 the artist left for his first visit to Afghanistan, which he subsequently returned to at least twice a year until the Soviet invasion of 1979. This radical decision had few precedents in the Italian art world, as he was one of the first artists who sought to immerse himself in a different culture through prolonged stays in a non-Western country. In September 1972 he opened the 'One Hotel' in Kabul, with his friend Dastaghir, mostly used by local tourists and by Boetti himself on his numerous stays. A series of photographs record these visits. They depict the inside of the hotel, the mountainous landscape surrounding the city and some scenes of daily life. Boetti's interest in Afghanistan has been cause of some of the most colourful speculations surrounding the artist's activities, and it is perhaps from these very images that we may find a clue as to his life-long fascination with its culture. The country's profoundly different customs, culture and landscape, the common-place use of drugs, allowed him to distance himself from that 'system' which the art of the period had challenged. In one of his few comments on Afghanistan, the artist wrote that "...my interest in all things distant had not been determined by my becoming an artist. I considered travel from a purely personal point of view, a hedonistic one. The main element of this attraction was quite specific: I was fascinated by the desert (and not only the one found in nature). Afghan homes, for example, are empty: no furniture therefore no objects commonly placed on furniture. There are only a few carpets and mattresses, cushions on which people lie down, drink, smoke and eat. I also like the fact that Afghans wear the same clothes at day and at night. I was most attracted to a sort of cancelling out, to desert civilisation. Afghanistan is a mountainous country, its villages are built on rocky flanks so as not to waste the fertile land of the valleys. Nothing has been added to the landscape: rocks are moved and used to build cube-houses, as in Paul Klee's watercolours, then a tree is pruned in order to make a load-bearing structure... The value that this type of society awards images is particularly extraordinary: a photograph of a garden, found in a copy of *Time* magazine, will be cut out and framed, behind glass, with some Sellotape. The resistance with which Afghans oppose our civilisation has always amazed me: nothing changes..."[32]

In Kabul, Boetti was introduced to the traditional local craft of embroidery. Photographs depicting the interior of the 'One Hotel' show small embroideries – rather than paintings - hung along the walls (fig. 11). Perhaps in response to these, the artist commissioned two square-shaped embroideries from local artisans. Each bears a date, set among a sophisticated floral design, corresponding to the title of the work: *16 dicembre 2040 11 luglio 2023* [16 December 2040 11 July 2023]. *16 dicembre...* marked a turning point in the artist's career, as the first of many tapestries produced continually in subsequent years. Once conceived, the execution was left to others. Also made in a wood and brass version, it is a playful example of the artist's interest in the temporal dimension of reality: the two dates refer respectively to the centenary of his birth and a guess as to his estimated year of death (fig. 39). Boetti was fascinated by concepts of time, a concern which runs through his entire production and that takes a variety of forms. The chimes of a bell tower opposite his studio in Rome dictated the marks made in *L'albero delle ore* [The Hour Tree], 1979, resulting in a series of symbols that record every quarter hour in the course of a day,

fig.11
Interior of 'One Hotel', Kabul, ca. 1972

fig.12
120 lettere dall'Afghanistan
[120 Letters From Afghanistan]
1972 (detail)
mixed media on paper, 120 stamped and franked envelopes
2 elements: each 132 x 120 cm and 1 element: 29.5 x 21 x 2.5 cm

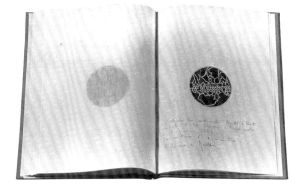

and form the work's structure (fig. 50). *Gli anni della mia vita* [The Years of My Life], 1976, more autobiographical in character, also renders the passing of time in visual form. Here the artist used a code that, when deciphered, reveals his age at the time of making the work (fig. 31). In other instances works were completed over a particularly extended period. These include *12 forme…*, *Orologio annuale* [Yearly Watch] which the artist made as an edition between 1977 and 1994 (fig. 15), and *Calendari* [Calendars], produced between 1978 and 1994 (fig. 57). "Time is fundamental, it is the main element in everything… the dates, the stamps and the squares are [for me] all ways of 'managing' time, which is the only truly magical thing that exists. It is incredibly elastic."[33]

In the course of his travels, from autumn 1970 onwards, Boetti commissioned a series of world maps (figs. 42, 43, 44 and 89). A seminal precedent for these works had been lace-pillow work titled *Territori occupati*, [Occupied Territories], 1969, devised by the artist and executed by Annemarie Sauzeau. The maps are large tapestries, in which the landmass of each country is marked by its respective national flag. According to the artist[34] and Annemarie Sauzeau, who traveled with him on his second trip to Kabul in September 1970,[35] the first of these maps was made by craftswomen who belonged to the school of a Mrs Kandi, and took more than a year to produce. Further maps were made between 1971 and 1973, each featuring small variations (such as different texts along the edges and a change in the colours used to depict Afghanistan). "…the embroidered map is for me the ultimate in beauty. I did nothing for that work. I chose nothing, in that the world is made the way it is, I did not draw it; flags are the way they are, I did not draw them; in other words I did absolutely nothing: once the basic idea has emerged, the concept, the rest is not a matter of choice…".[36] The manufacturing of several maps marked the start of a purposefully 'abundant' production which Boetti, in contrast to the notion of a 'unique work', provocatively adopted as a systematic principle throughout his entire practice: "…from that moment onwards I moved in an opposite direction: towards profusion, seriality…"[37]

In the autumn of 1972 Boetti moved from Turin, with its close-knit artistic community, to the disparate and complex cultural networks of Rome. Its more explicitly Mediterranean culture was undoubtedly close to Boetti's own outlook, yet the artist always referred to himself as an outsider, with a displaced sense of belonging. Once in Rome, he took a studio close to Piazza Santa Maria in Trastevere and started on a new type of work, co-ordinated by Maria Angelica De Gaetano. Throughout this series, derived from hatching with a ball-point pen, the artist only provided a text and a visual structure, leaving the execution of each piece to others. In this way, Maria Angelica De Gaetano involved people who did not necessarily belong to the art world: "…I chose people from various neighbourhoods, of all ages, and each worked in a different way. The only rule they had to observe was that they couldn't leave too many white areas on the sheet of paper. Otherwise, everyone was free to work as they chose…so that some drew larger lines, others more rigid ones, others still drew in a mechanical way, thinking, dreaming…a little like automatic writing…Alighiero often didn't want to know who had worked on a particular sheet of paper…he liked to guess…he could distinguish a woman's stroke …Then he'd ask me who they were and what they did in life…"[38] As is often the case with Boetti, the meaning of these 'biro' works is organised around a system the viewer needs to 'unlock'. The key, in this instance, lies in tracking floating commas against the letters of the Latin alphabet, arranged either along the top or left-hand side of each sheet of paper. The words or phrases revealed spell out the title of the work, and reflect some of the artist's fundamental concerns: *Mettere al mondo il mondo* [To Give Birth to the World], 1972-1973, (fig. 88)[39] *I sei sensi* [The Six Senses], 1973 (fig. 40), *Languidi sguardi assassini* [Languid Murderous Glances], 1974, *La luce della notte* [Night's Light], ca. 1974, *Dare tempo al tempo* [To Give Time Time], 1982. In one of the earliest examples of this type of work, *ABEEGHIIILOORTT*, 1971-72, Boetti rearranged the letters of his name in alphabetical order.

The relationship between 'order' and 'disorder' is one of the fundamental categories, based on bipolarity, on which Boetti's entire thought process rests (full and empty, half and double, adding and subtracting, multiplication and division and so on). It represents a personal response to the positivist attitude that typifies Western philosophy, still firmly

fig.13*
Cimento dell'armonia e dell'invenzione
[Contest Between Harmony and Invention]
1969
pencil on squared paper
25 elements: each 70 x 50 cm
Galleria 1000 Eventi, Milan

fig.14*
Giorgio Colombo
1973
ball point pen on paper
22 x 18 cm
Giorgio Colombo collection, Milan

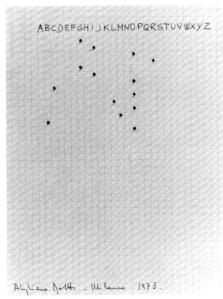

rooted in unitarian thought.[40] The first work to explore this relationship was *Ordine e Disordine* [Order and Disorder], 1971-1972, a template that when temporarily placed over a wall and sprayed with green paint, forms the words of the title directly onto the wall. The words are arranged in successive vertical lines to create a square grid, and the number of letters – 16 – corresponds to those in 'Alighiero e Boetti'. Subsequent versions of this work were produced as embroideries. *Ordine e disordine*, 1973, consists of 100 small tapestries hung in a square configuration, while *Order and Disorder*, 1985-1986, comprises 199 tapestries (fig. 52).

Boetti derived the grid structure of these works from the Oriental concept of 'magical squares' [in Italian 'squared phrases'], in which words or phrases are arranged in a similar manner. He developed the system in an abundant production of tapestries, featuring equally abundant sayings and aphorisms that stemmed from diverse cultural, philosophical, mathematical and linguistic contexts, as well as from the artist's more personal experience of everyday life. "I drew about 150 pairs of words which could be arranged in a square. Nowadays, when I come across a particular expression such as 'Your inner strength' (a Yoga principle), I instinctively know whether the letters which make up the phrase can be arranged in a square. Each of these pieces was produced in an edition of 100. But each varies in colour and in the particular style adopted by the craftswoman who made it. It is therefore neither an original work nor a multiple..."[41] Boetti's emphasis on each letter's individual meaning and, more generally, his investigation into the complex nature of linguistic systems, closely relate to his study of Oriental cultures. Sufism was a particularly strong influence[42], and in 1979 the artist became a pupil of Berang Ramazan, a Sufi Master.[43]

Boetti's first two solo exhibitions in the United States were held in 1974, at John Weber Gallery and Sperone Gallery in New York. These coincided with his participation to *Eight Contemporary Artists*, held at the Museum of Modern Art, which proposed the work of a number of artists considered to be amongst the most interesting to have emerged in the late sixties and early seventies. Boetti, who was the only Italian artist to be included, exhibited *Mettere al mondo il mondo* and showed alongside Vito Acconci, Daniel Buren, Hanne Darboven, Jan Dibbets, Robert Hunter, Brice Marden and Dorothea Rockburne. The show was poorly received by critics, and Boetti featured in few of the reviews. Between 1974 and 1976 the artist travelled to Ethiopia, Sudan and Guatemala (where he took a series of photographs later used in *Guatemala*, 1974-1975, fig. 75). Francesco Clemente, who formed a lasting friendship with Boetti on his arrival in Rome in 1970, joined him on one of his trips to Afghanistan in 1976. He has recently acknowledged the profound influence Boetti had on him at the outset of his career, [44] and once said of him: "…Alighiero, it is easy to learn from you. It is difficult to stay your friend. In your relations you are a born gambler, always doubling the stakes. But, yes, to be a gambler is so consistent with your worldview: a permutating field of possibilities. A chaotic weave of contrasting colours..."[45]

In his early postal works, Boetti had already begun to turn his attention towards the world of mathematics. This became more explicit in a series of works made between 1975 and 1977, which directly referred to laws governing numerical progression, combinational possibilities, and to the potential for rapid acceleration that is implicit in multiplication. These include *Da Mille a Mille* [From One Thousand to One Thousand] (fig. 49), *Storia naturale della moltiplicazione* [Natural History of Multiplication] (fig. 92), *La quadratura del Mille* [The Squaring of One Thousand] and *Alternando da uno a cento e viceversa* [Alternating One to One Hundred and Vice Versa] (figs. 59, 63 and 93). For Boetti numbers, like letters, were characterised by individual personalities, and always held particular symbolic values: "Numbers are the only real entity in the universe, the only one that exists autonomously. If it is true that we have, by convention, placed B after A, it is not necessarily by convention that we place 2 after 1…Each has its own individuality, its own presence: like perhaps 3 is Master 3, 2 recalls the concept of dualism, of the double, 1 is the unit, 4 is the earth, the four walls..."[46]

In 1979 Boetti's mother died. He dedicated *Regno Musicale* [Musical Kingdom] to her (fig. 32), a drawing that alludes to her lifelong interest in music. He also referred to his mother in an untitled postal work (fig. 45), composed of 14 envelopes and a text that poetically remembers her, placed at the centre of the piece and written by the artist with his left hand. First used in the Munich

fig.15*
Orologio annuale
[Yearly Watch]
1977
wristwatch, limited edition
4.3 cm diameter
Courtesy Agata Boetti, Paris

fig.16*
Classificazione dei mille fiumi più lunghi del mondo
[Classifying the Thousand Longest Rivers of the World]
1970-1977
book, 1018 pages; edition of 500
21.5 x 16.5 x 5.5 cm
version with embroidered cover
Collection Annemarie Sauzeau Boetti, Paris

performance of 1970, he adopted this practice in many of his drawings on paper of the 1980s. From 1976 to the early 80s the production of commissioned works intensified, leading to works such as *Faccine* [Little Faces], 1979, a black and white poster designed by the artist and coloured in by a group of children. During this period the artist also made partly autobiographical works, such as *Gli anni della mia vita* [The Years of My Life], 1976, (fig. 31) and *Collo rotto braccia Lunghe* [Broken Neck Long Arms], 1976-1977. At the same time *Gary Gilmore*, 1977 and later, as from 1983, a series of drawings which traced magazine covers (*Anno*), reflect the artist's continuing interest in the stories and images of daily life and current affairs. *Gary Gilmore* (figs. 18 and 94) focuses on the case of an American murderer who demanded to be sentenced to death, rather than live out a life sentence in prison (the work also depicts Pier Paolo Pasolini's body), [47] while in the *Anno* series, each cover depicts disparate information, styles and images unified by the homogeneous mark of a pencil (fig. 58). Between 16 December 1980 and 24 April 1981 the artist collaborated with the left-wing daily newspaper *Il Manifesto*, which each day during this period published a different drawing by the artist on the front page.

In the early 1980s Boetti developed a series of works entitled *La natura, una faccenda ottusa* [Nature, A Dumb Affair][48] which became a recurring theme throughout the decade (fig. 86). He said of these works: "I wanted to present an image of nature as a reality without shapes or colours, as a senseless running towards life…" "I think that one of our culture's most glaring mistakes has been to divide the world into rigid classifications, such as animals, vegetables and minerals etc. I think this division is a mental category that blurs, veils the possibility of understanding things."[49] In the same period the artist also participated in two contrasting group exhibitions, *Identité Italienne: L'Art en Italie depuis 1959* at the Centre Georges Pompidou, and *Avanguardia Transavanguardia*, held at the Mure Aureliane in Rome. The Paris exhibition, curated by Celant, was the first in a series of historic revisitations of Arte Povera within the context of Italian art between 1960 and 1980. The second, curated by Achille Bonito Oliva, reflected a new tendency brought together under the banner of 'Transavanguardia'. In contrast to previous avant-garde movements and in conformity with post-modern theory, Bonito Oliva proposed an art typified by mobility, eclecticism and a nomadism of ideas and images.

The production of embroidered works had decreased in regularity during this period, following the Soviet invasion of Afghanistan in 1979. In 1984 Boetti resumed his collaboration with the Afghan weavers, who had sought refuge in Peshawar, Pakistan, and with them began work on a new series. These works, titled *Tutto* [Everything], were derived by embroidering large fabrics, on which the artist's assistants had already traced numerous images taken from disparate sources: animal encyclopaedias, newspapers, drawings of oriental miniatures and so on (fig. 56). Each version was always undertaken with 100 differently coloured threads, all of equal length. The formal precedents for these works date back to Boetti's early career – they can be found in an untitled drawing from 1967, for example[50] - and to later key works like *120 lettere dall'Afghanistan*[51] [120 Letters From Afghanistan], 1972, (fig. 12) and *Perdita d'identità*[52] [Loss of Identity], 1980. The ideas at the root of *Tutto* may perhaps best be observed in *Pack*, 1967. This consisted of a cylindrical container, filled with liquid cement that, when left to dry, formed a cracked surface: "*Pack* is, for Boetti, the primordial and unitary representation of the world, a solid mass similar to the ice packs found along the Danish coast, which consist of large sheets of ice that are more or less welded to each other. A drifting and almost dislocated puzzle, which slowly emerges and proliferates – like splitting cells, or tectonic plates…".[53] *Tutto* emerges from a vision of the world in which everything meets. It also presents a notion of 'fullness', understood as the ability to encompass everything, as the desire to dissolve one's own self (*Perdita d'identità*) in the indistinct flow of life and its countless fragments. This movement towards an incessant proliferation of images is echoed in a series of 80s drawings called *Extra-strong*, culminating with a frieze made for the Venice Biennale of 1990. The frieze occupied the entire length of the room Boetti was exhibiting in, and presented a succession of compositional elements that included the artist's handwriting, drawn with his left hand, the outline of various animals, shapes derived from the use of masks, the imprint

fig.17
Autoritratto
[Self-portrait]
1993
bronze, electrical and hydraulic attachments
205 x 90 x 60 cm
Installation at Sonsbeek '93

fig.18*
Gary Gilmore
1977
Indian ink on paper
2 elements: each 100 x 150 cm
Achille and Ida Maramotti Collection, Albinea

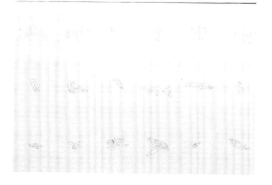

of seals collected by the artist since his first trip to Afghanistan, and much more. Taken as a whole, the frieze created a feeling of unstoppable flux that was, for the artist, the essence of life itself. "Perhaps I wanted to talk about the density, the richness that exists in the world, which can be revealed through attentive and analytical observation, one that is equally rich, equally multi-faceted. I wanted to talk about the enormous quantity of human products: products of intelligence, of curiosity, of attentiveness. In truth, I could talk about a thousand things."[54]

In 1989 Boetti participated in *Magiciens de la Terre*, held at the Centre Pompidou in Paris. The show, which aimed to draw parallels between works by artists from a large variety of nationalities and heterogeneous cultures, was one of the most controversial to be held in the late eighties. Boetti exhibited a tapestry, *Poesie con il Sufi Berang* [Poems with the Sufi Berang], 1988-1989, which features a poem by the Sufi Master Berang Ramazan in Farsi, the Persian language also spoken in Afghanistan. In Paris he met various artists from non-Western cultures, including Frédéric Bruly-Bouabré, from the Ivory Cost, with whom he discovered a number of shared interests. In 1993 - together with his second wife, Caterina Raganelli and his son Giordano – the artist travelled to Africa and visited Zéprégühé, Bruly-Bouabré's home town. Together they started work on an exhibition at the DIA Centre for the Arts in New York (titled *World Envisioned – Alighiero e Boetti, Frédéric Bruly-Bouabré*), scheduled for October 1994. Boetti died a few months before the exhibition opened.

A large retrospective, titled *De bouche à oreille*, was held toward the end of the artist's career at Le Magasin in Grenoble. For the exhibition, he commissioned 50 kilims from Pakistan, based on the theme of *Alternando da uno a cento e viceversa* (fig. 63). This was a large collective work, one that involved more than twenty weavers and students from several French fine art colleges, who designed the preparatory cartoons within a system set by the artist. For the same exhibition, Boetti also made his largest postal work, *Oeuvre Postal* [Postal Work], 1993, completed with the help of the Musée de la Poste in Paris. Works such as these reveal the artist's desire to adopt a similar role to an orchestra's conductor: "…I have just held an exhibition in Milan and the following morning [sic] I brought all my assistants together. This to me was further confirmation of my desire to work like a film director: with [camera] operators, a photographer, editing, an organised task force…".[55]

On the other hand, during these last years, Boetti also returned to a more personal, autobiographical subject, one of the recurring vehicles through which he explored his philosophical outlook. In a bronze sculpture titled *Autoritratto* [Self Portrait], 1993, water is carried through a tube held by the figure's right hand, and transformed into steam by the heat emanating from its body (fig. 17). This process of transformation, as though generated by his own creative energy, once again alludes to the artist as a shaman or magic demiurge, as with the earlier poster work titled *Shaman Showman*. If *Autoritratto* presents the figure of the artist with a sculptural solidity, in other works the image almost completely disappears, as though nullifying itself. *Sedia* [Chair], 1990, depicts the delicate outline of a series of strictly self-referential objects: a chair, a bamboo stick and the red imprint of a seal the artist wore as a ring (fig. 55). In *Vento* [Wind], made a few years earlier (1985), shapes seem to have completely disappeared, the image virtually cancelled out by a technique the artist learnt from a Japanese calligrapher and he termed 'massage on paper' (fig. 19). When read from a Western perspective the black marks convey a sense of lightness and of speed, two qualities that were particularly dear to Boetti. "Wind is a moment of grace. The shapes created by wind are always ones of energy, of movement. Wind, furthermore, makes things temporary, and also conveys a sense of time, because through it succession, instant after instant, is rendered in shapes…it is a real force, alive, like the sun's rays, but lighter, even if its energy at times can be extremely violent. But its image remains one of lightness, even mentally: words that are light, that are airy…"[56]

Antonella Soldaini

fig.19*
Vento
[Wind]
1985
ink on mounted paper
140 x 72 cm
Collection Caterina Boetti, Rome

Footnotes

1   Alighiero e Boetti, 'A Text for Frédéric', in *Alighiero e Boetti, Frédéric Bruly Bouabré, World Envisioned*, exh. cat., Dia Centre for the Arts, New York, 6 October 1994 – 25 June 1995, p. 96

2   Mirella Bandini, 'Intervista ad Alighiero Boetti', *NAC*, n. 3, Rome, March 1973. Reprinted in *Alighiero Boetti*, exh. cat., Galleria Civica d'Arte Moderna, Turin, 10 May – 1 September 1996, p. 200.

3   Boetti later always referred to this work as *Cartone ondulato*.

4   The artist subsequently adopted the title *Zig Zag* for this work.

5   Alighiero Boetti, untitled text written for his first solo exhibition at Christian Stein Gallery, 1967. Reprinted in exh. cat. Turin, 1996, p. 99.

6   M. Bandini, op. cit., p. 203

7   Germano Celant, 'Arte Povera – Im spazio', in *Arte Povera – Im Spazio*, exh. cat., Galleria La Bertesca, Genoa, 27 September – 20 October 1967. Translation by Paul Blanchard in *Arte Povera*, Electa Editrice, Milan, 1985, pp. 31-33.

8   Germano Celant, *Arte Povera*, Electa Editrice, Milan, 1985, pp. 30-31

9   Germano Celant, 'Per i ciechi tutto è improvviso', in *Alighiero Boetti*, exh. cat., Galleria La Bertesca, Genoa, December 1967

10 Boetti talked about *Manifesto* in: M. Bandini, op. cit., p. 211.

11 Carolyn Christov-Bakargiev's supposition that Boetti's heirs have attempted to hide the key has not been substantiated (cf. Carolyn Christov-Bakargiev (ed.), *Arte Povera*, Phaidon Press, London, 1999).

12 Germano Celant, 'Arte Povera. Appunti per una guerriglia', *Flash Art*, n. 5, Milan, November/December 1967, p. 3

13 Gabriele Perretta, 'L'arte, gli artisti e il '68', *Flash Art*, n.147, Milan, December 1988/January 1989, p. 69

14 The work can be seen in the short film, *Boettiinbiancoenero* [Boettiinblackandwhite], filmed by Ugo Nespolo on the day of the opening.

15 Eliphas Lévi, *Histoire de la Magie*, Editions Germer Baillière, Paris, 1860

16 According to Corrado Levi, a very close friend of Boetti's at the time, the artist also referred to this work as *Aiuola* (Flower Bed).

17 In his interview with Mirella Bandini (op. cit., p. 202) he mentioned a project for a *Parco Magico* (Magical Park).

18 Giovan Battista Salerno, 'Manuale di Conoscenza', in *Alighiero e Boetti*, exh. cat., Le Nouveau Musée, Villeurbanne, Lyon, 7 February – 20 April 1986

19 Achille Bonito Oliva, 'Alighiero Boetti', in *Dialoghi d'artista. Incontri con l'arte contemporanea. 1970 – 1984*, Electa Editrice, Milan, 1984. Reprinted in exh. cat. Turin, 1996, p. 211.

20 M. Bandini, op. cit., p. 200

21 In: *Avvenimenti 7. Alighiero e Boetti*, programme made by Marco Giusti for RAI, Radio Televisione Italiana, 1996

22 G. Perretta, op. cit., p. 69

23 A. Bonito Oliva, op. cit., p. 208

24 On the invitation to the exhibition, the title for the work is 'Io prendo il sole a Torino il 24-2-1969'. From the mid-seventies this changes to 'Io che prendo il sole a Torino il 19 gennaio 1969'.

25 This work was subsequently titled *Niente da vedere niente da nascondere* [Nothing to See Nothing to Hide].

26 Annemarie Sauzeau Boetti, *Classifying the thousand longest rivers of the world*, 1970-1977

27 For a more detailed description of the work cf. Diletta Borromeo's *Technical Notes on the works of Alighiero Boetti* in this catalogue.

28 For an analysis of the relationship between the two artists cf. *Origine et Destination. Alighiero e Boetti, Douglas Huebler*, Société des Expositions du Palais des Beaux-Arts, Brussels, 1997

29 Sol LeWitt, 'Paragraphs on Conceptual Art', *Artforum*, New York, June 1967. Reprinted in *Sol LeWitt*, The Museum of Modern Art, New York, 1978, pp. 166-167.

30 For a more detailed account of the book's influence on Boetti's thinking cf. Maria Teresa Roberto, 'Alighiero Boetti 1966-1970, le parole le cose' in exh. cat. Turin, 1996, p. 31

31 Boetti made a number of drawings based on this concept. Reproduced in exh. cat. Turin, 1996, p. 34.

32 Nicolas Bourriaud, 'Afghanistan', *Documents*, n.1, Paris, October 1992, pp. 50-51

33 A. Bonito Oliva, op. cit., p. 209. For the importance of the concept of time in Boetti's practice, cf. also Jean-Christophe Ammann, 'Dare tempo al tempo', in exh. cat. Turin, 1996, pp. 15-21

34 N. Bourriaud, op. cit., p. 52

35 A. Sauzeau, 'Alighiero e Boetti, una vita', in exh. cat. Turin, 1996, p. 248

36 Alighiero Boetti in exh. cat. Turin, 1996, p. 199. The first map to be shown in Italy was reproduced on the cover of the May 1972 issue of *Data* magazine, while the first exhibitions in which the works were shown date back to 1973 (at Galleria Toselli, Milan and Galleria Sperone Fischer, Rome).

37 N. Bourriaud, op. cit., p. 53

38 Unpublished interview, December 1998

39 Translator's note: the title literally translates as 'To put the world into the world', 'to put into the world' meaning 'to give birth' in Italian.

40 For further information on the relationship between Boetti's work and Western thought cf. Rolf Lauter, 'Order and disorder', in *Alighiero Boetti: Mettere al mondo il mondo*, exh. cat., Museum für Moderne Kunst, Frankfurt, 30 January – 10 May 1998, pp. 97-109

41 N. Bourriaud, op. cit., pp. 53-54

42 Boetti undertook extensive research into the history of his ancestor Giovan Battista Boetti, a monk who lived in the 18th century and who converted to Sufism in 1743. Some of the documents that he was able to collect contributed to *Giovan Battista Boetti. 1743/1798*, OEMME Edizioni, Milan, 1989.

43 For Boetti's relationship with Eastern culture cf. 'Shirazeh Houshiary in conversation with Mario Codognato' in this catalogue and Caterina Maderna-Lauter, 'The Fusion of East and West – The Unity of Yesterday and Today', in exh. cat. Frankfurt, 1998, pp. 267-299.

44 For an account of Boetti's relationship to Francesco Clemente cf. Francesco Clemente, 'Apricots and Pomegranates', in exh. cat. New York, 1994-95, pp. 61-62 and also 'Conversazione tra Francesco Clemente, Danilo Eccher e Francesco Pellizzi', in *Francesco Clemente, opere su carta*, Villa delle Rose, Bologna, 12 September – 29 May 1999, pp. 27-29.

45 F. Clemente, op. cit., p. 61

46 Bruno Corà, 'Alighiero Boetti – Un disegno del pensiero che va', *A.E.I.U.O.*, n. 6, December 1982. Reprinted in *Alighiero Boetti*, exh. cat. Turin, 1996, p. 209.

47 Pier Paolo Pasolini, one of the most important intellectuals in post war Italian culture, was murdered in 1975.

48 The title was taken from a text written by the English philosopher and mathematician, Alfred North Whitehead.

49 Sergio Lombardi (ed.), *Alighiero e Boetti, Dall'oggi al domani*, Edizioni L'Obliquo, Brescia, pp. 17/29

50 Reproduced in exh. cat. Turin, 1996, p. 41

51 Ibid., pp. 130-131

52 Ibid., p. 43

53 A. Sauzeau, 'Gli undici sensi', in exh. cat. Turin, 1996, p. 41

54 S. Lombardi (ed.), op. cit., p. 14

55 Anna Mattirolo, 'Tutto', in *Alighiero e Boetti. L'opera Ultima*, exh. cat., Galleria Nazionale d'Arte Moderna, Rome, 16 December 1996 – 27 April 1997, p. 47

56 S. Lombardi (ed.), op. cit., p. 21

fig.21*
Scala
[Ladder]
1966
wood
172 x 111 x 47 cm
Christian Stein Collection, Turin

opposite
fig.20*
Niente da vedere niente da nascondere
[Nothing to See Nothing to Hide]
1969 (1986)
iron and glass
300 x 400 cm
Collection Agata Boetti, Paris and Matteo Boetti, Rome

fig.22*
Lampada annuale
[Yearly Lamp]
ca. 1966
wood, metal, glass, electric mechanism
78.1 x 40 x 40 cm
Private collection

fig.23*
Ping Pong
1966
painted wood, glass, electric mechanism
2 elements: each 50 x 50 x 20 cm
Goetz Collection, Munich

fig.24*
Tavelle
[Tiles]
1967
firebricks
110 x 110 x 6 cm ca.
Celant Collection, Genoa

fig.25*
Iter-vallo
1969 (1993)
iron and tissue paper
93 x 93 x 1cm
Private collection, London
The title is a play on words that refer to
concepts of union and of separation:
intervallo [interval], iter [path] and vallo
[to pass through something]

fig.26*
Io che prendo il sole a Torino il 19 gennaio 1969
[Me Sunbathing in Turin on 19 January 1969]
1969
quick-setting cement, cabbage butterfly
177 x 90 cm ca.
Private collection, Turin

fig.27*
Legnetti colorati
[Small Coloured Sticks]
1968
painted wood and rubber
diameter 150 cm
Private collection

fig.28*
Zig Zag
1966
fabric and aluminium
50 x 50 x 50 cm
Christian Stein Collection, Turin

opposite
fig.29*
Senza titolo
[Untitled]
1966
plastic and aluminium
50 x 100 cm ca.
N. Trentalance

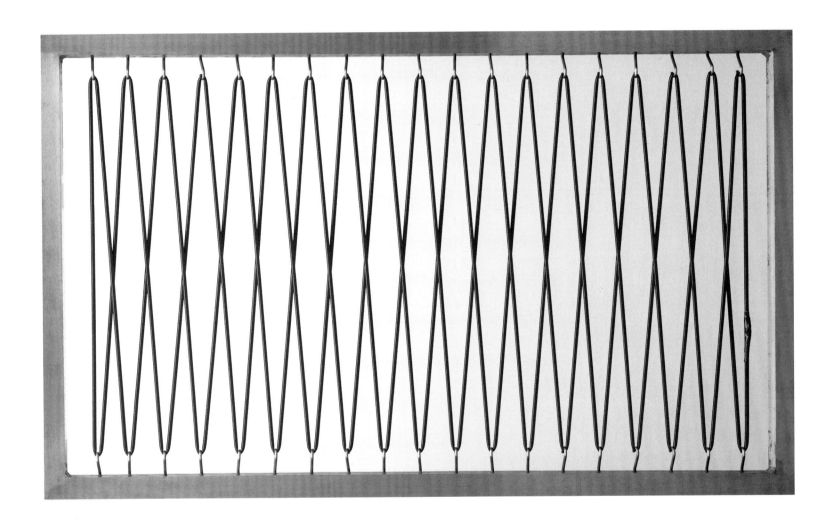

fig.30*
Manifesto
1967 + 1970
print on paper, produced in 7 different colours
from an edition of 800 printed in 1967
50 signed and numbered in1970
100 x 70 cm
ed. 15/50
Colombo Collection, Milan

opposite left
fig.31*
Gli anni della mia vita
[The Years of My Life]
1976
ink on paper
104 x 75 cm
Collection Matteo Boetti, Rome

opposite right
fig.32*
Regno Musicale
[Musical Kingdom]
1979
pencil on mounted paper
150 x 100 cm
Collection Annemarie Sauzeau Boetti, Paris

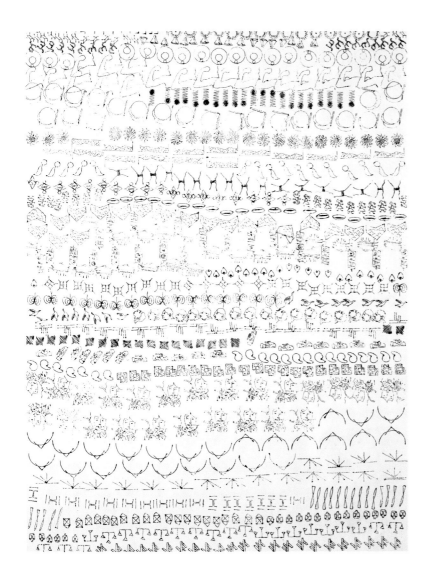

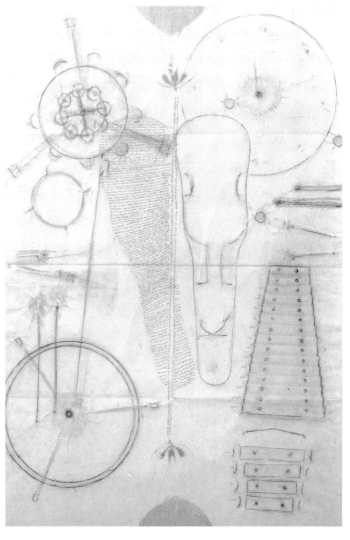

fig.33*
The Thin Thumb
1966
paint and varnish on wood and cork
50 x 50 x 8 cm
Monika Sprüth / Pasquale Leccese

fig.34*
Stiff Upper Lip
1966
paint and varnish on wood and cork
90 x 70 cm
Christian Stein Collection, Turin

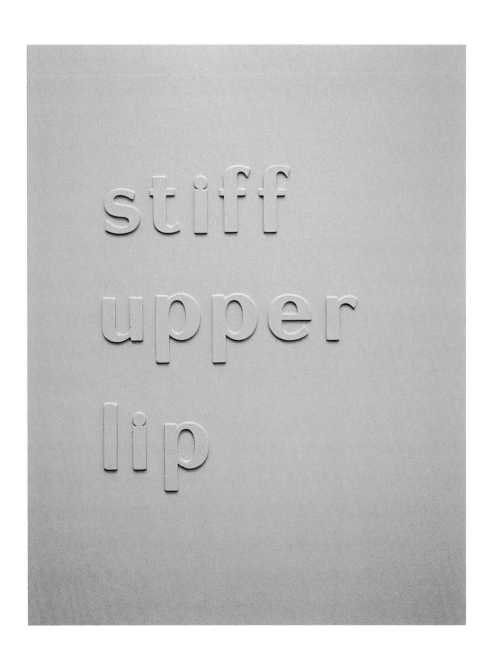

fig.35*
Mimetico
[Camouflage]
1966
camouflage fabric
170 x 270 cm
Christian Stein Collection, Turin

fig.36*
Millenovecentosettanta
[N-i-n-e-t-e-e-n-s-e-v-e-n-t-y]
1970
cast iron and spray paint
35 x 35 x 2 cm ca.
Goetz Collection, Munich

fig.37*
Senza titolo
[Untitled]
ca. 1973
collage on paper
55 x 45 cm
Collection Bruno van Lierde, Brussels

fig.38*
Calligrafia
[Handwriting]
1971
ink on paper
70 x 70 cm
Paolo and Alida Giuli

opposite
fig.39*
16 dicembre 2040 11 luglio 2023
[16 December 2040 11 July 2023]
1971
embroidery
2 elements: each 50 x 50 cm
Gian Enzo Sperone, New York

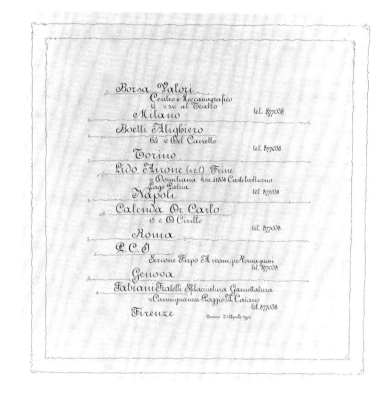

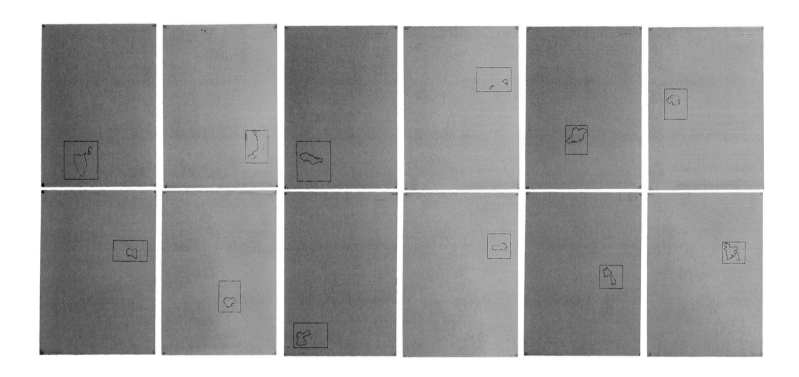

fig.40*
I sei sensi
[The Six Senses]
1973
blue ball point pen on mounted paper
11 elements: each 150 x 110 cm
Collection Helmut Schmelzer, Nürnberg

opposite
fig.41*
12 forme dal 10 giugno 1967
[12 Shapes from 10 June 1967]
1967-1971
copper etching
12 elements: each 59 x 43 cm
Private collection, Rome

fig.42*
Mappa
[Map]
1989-1992
embroidery
255 x 580 cm
Collection Giordano Boetti, Rome

fig.43*
Mappa
[Map]
1988
embroidery
115 x 213 cm
Collection Caterina Boetti, Rome

opposite
fig.44*
Mappa
[Map]
1971-1973
embroidery
230 x 380 cm
Collection Annemarie Sauzeau Boetti,
Paris

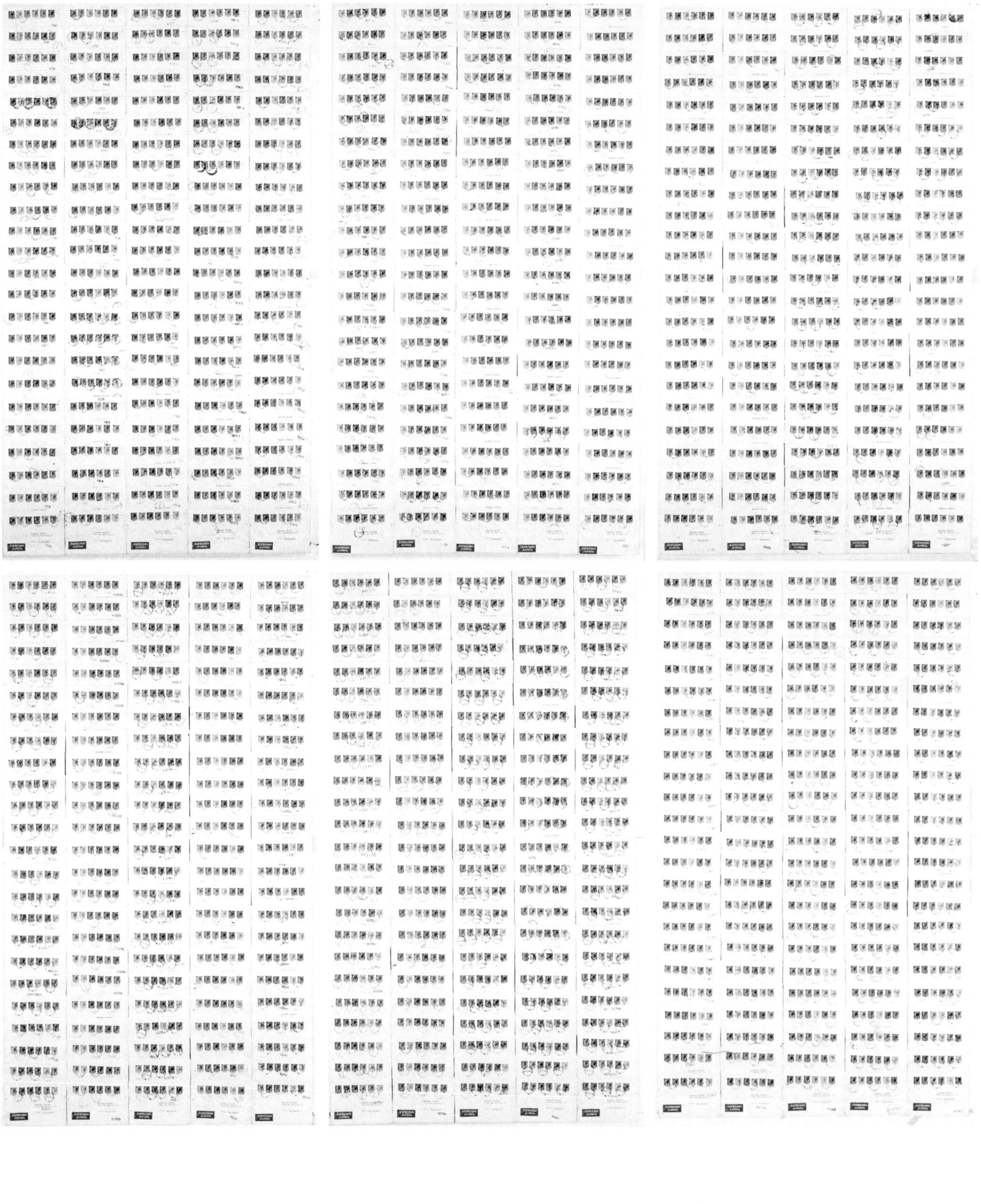

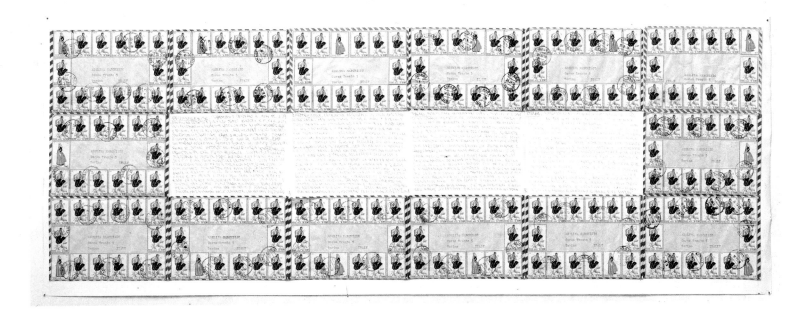

fig.45*
Senza titolo
[Untitled]
1979
mixed media on paper, 14 stamped
and franked envelopes
30 x 126 cm
Collection Annemarie Sauzeau Boetti,
Paris

opposite
fig.46*
Senza numero I-VI
[Un-numbered I-VI]
1972
mixed media on paper, 720 stamped
and franked envelopes
6 elements: each 144.5 x 86 cm
Stedelijk Museum, Amsterdam

fig.47*
I vedenti
[The Sighted]
1972-1973
embroidery
174 x 150 cm
Gino Viliani collection

opposite
fig.48*
Addizione
[Adding Up]
1984
embroidery
201 x 198.5 cm.
Collection Roberto Casamonti, Florence

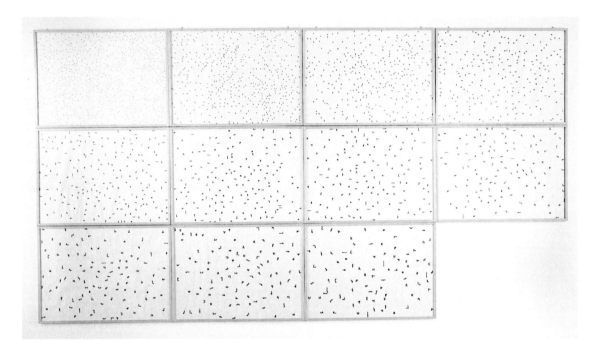

fig.49*
Da mille a mille
[From One Thousand to One Thousand]
1975
ink on squared paper
11 elements: each 70 x 100 cm
Christian Stein Collection, Turin

fig.50*
L'albero delle ore
[The Hour Tree]
1979
embroidery
325 x 193 cm
Monika Sprüth / Pasquale Leccese

fig.51*
Aerei
[Aeroplanes]
1977
watercolour and pencil
on mounted paper
3 elements: each 140 x 100 cm
Christian Stein Collection, Turin

fig.52*
Order and Disorder
1985-1986
embroidery
199 elements: each 17 x 17 cm
Museum für Moderne Kunst,
Frankfurt am Main
Acquired with the help of the ARS
EUROPA Foundation and with donations
from the Friends of the Museums für
Moderne Kunst e. V.

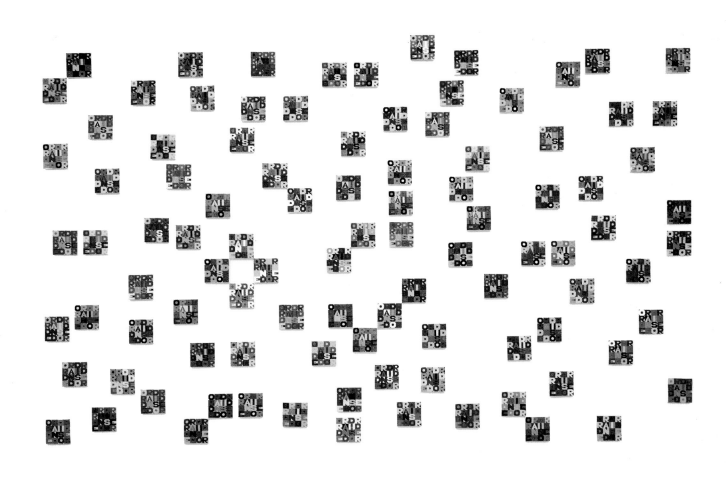

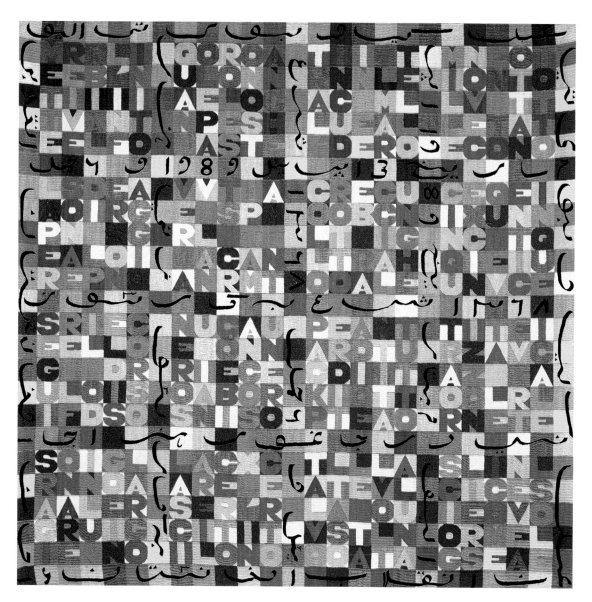

fig.53*
Senza titolo
[Untitled]
1988
embroidery
110 x 110 cm
Galleria Seno, Milan

opposite left
fig.54*
Arti-colazioni
[Articulations]
1984
tempera and ink on mounted paper
4 elements: each 100 x 70 cm
Collection Matteo Boetti, Rome

opposite right
fig.55*
Senza titolo
[Untitled]
1990
pencil and tempera on mounted
paper
270 x 310 cm
Collection Chiara and Francesco
Carraro

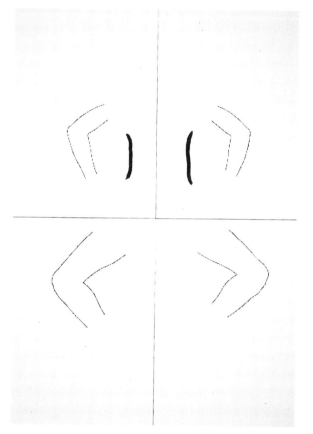

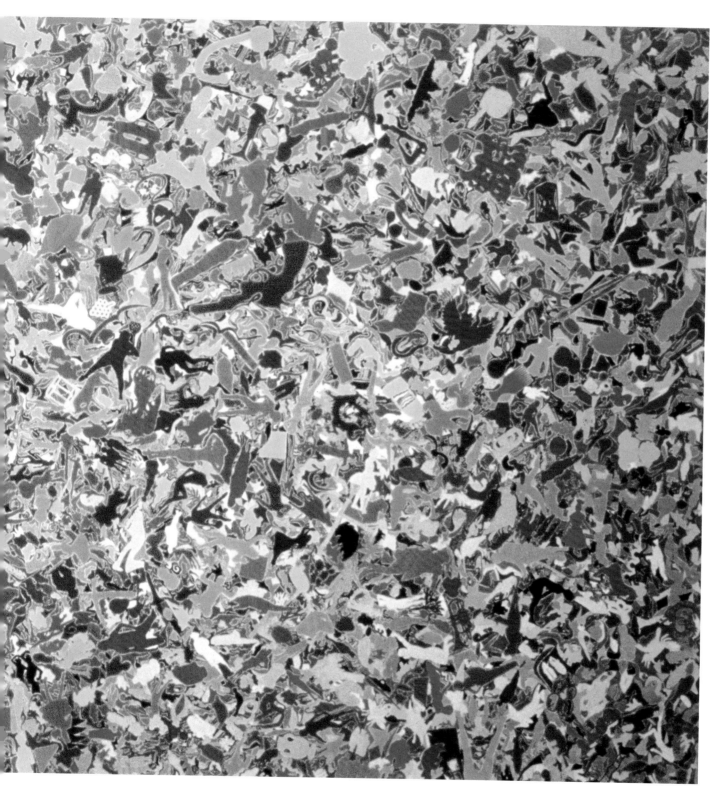

fig.56*
Tutto
[Everything]
ca. 1989
embroidery
445 x 227 cm
Collection Annemarie Sauzeau Boetti,
Paris

fig.57*
Calendario
[Calendar]
1990
collage and pencil on paper
27 x 37 cm
Collection Maria Angelica De Gaetano,
Rome (The calendar for 1984 has been
kindly lent by Giovan Battista Salerno,
Rome)
Detail of an installation consisting of 17
works, of variable dimensions. One was
made each year between 1978 and 1994.

opposite
fig.58*
Anno 1990
[Year 1990]
1990
pencil on mounted paper
12 elements: each 100 x 100 cm
Collection Giordano Boetti, Rome

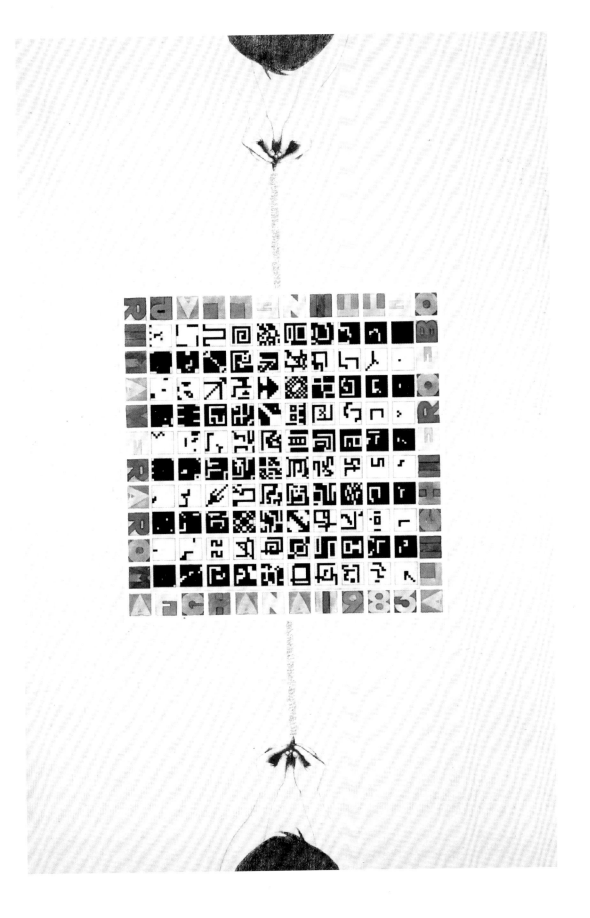

fig.59*
**Alternando da uno a cento e
viceversa**
[Alternating One to One Hundred and
Vice Versa]
1982-1983
mixed media on mounted paper
150 x 100 cm
Louise and Eric Franck, London

Alighiero, Boetti, and the Others

Alighiero and Boetti

When I first met him, Alighiero Boetti was intent on memorising the alphabet, from Z to A. I do not know whether he ever completed this work, which was neither an object nor an image. Another time, he mentioned to me that one day he had seen a young man waving to him from a window, that the window was a window in his own house, and that the man was himself.

Between these two small occurrences, one of them abstract, the other figurative, there exists a connection less tenuous than the occurrences themselves, one immediately encountered in Boetti's work. I shall try to make this absolutely clear. A given order must have its opposite, which is not necessarily disorder. A given sequence, a series in order, is one which we must be able to follow in both directions. A given image must necessarily have some reality or other, however distant, from which the image has been detached, and, conversely, there is no image whose origins do not lie in some gap in reality, albeit a minimal one. Which means that the first of the two occurrences is not an overthrowing, and the second is not a form of schizophrenia. The *Gemelli* [Twins] (fig.6) - from 1968 - are not an image of the Doppelganger; after all, they are walking hand in hand in the shade of a tree-lined avenue, and not in the darkness of some subterranean landscape of the psyche. As for the "alphabetical countdown", it is worth formulating a conjecture. There is a part of language that language does not reach, but which is not the same as silence. It is like the left-hand[1] side[2] of language, its blind side.[3] In all of his work, Boetti rebuts this as conjecture, converting it into a proof. Starting out with some very "French" years of theorising on this question, he conducted a ceaseless pursuit of whatever is to be found on the underside of the obsessive arbitrariness of language, and instead of finding the Other of language, or at least an other language, he found ten thousand others.

One of the purposes of this note is to trace to what extent the concept of the Double was developed in Boetti's work, how this concept, this idea or this metaphor became a method, and with what results (when Alberto Savinio wrote "Maupassant and the other", for example, the concept had not yet entirely cast off certain pathological associations). The other purpose of this note - which, while presuming to play around a bit with words and ideas, includes only two of them - is to make a point, for once, about the fundamentally plain and traditional character of the work of a revolutionary artist. But it is to be hoped that we shall achieve this second purpose with more simplicity, touching on it and no more.

The others

Frédéric Bruly Bouabré. Ivory Coast, Abidjan. "A negro of purple race".
At dawn on Thursday 11 March 1948, the Heavenly God appeared to him in a splendid solar vision. He became a prophet, a member of the Order of the Persecuted, taking the name Cheik Nadro-le-Révélateur. In October 1994, the Dia Center for the Arts in New York put on an exhibition about his meeting with Alighiero Boetti. And it was an amazing exhibition, even though Alighiero, who had done a lot of work preparing for it, was no longer here to see it. In the catalogue, though, there is a text in which Boetti sets out with great clarity his ideas and reflections on so-called "Negro Art". These ideas differ from the ones Picasso had.

Azam Mazari. Master carpet-weaver. Carpet Centre, Naz Cinema Road, Peshawar, Pakistan.
"Under my astrakhan cap a computer hums away".
"A man who smokes hashish must by necessity be an honest man".
 For Mr Alighiero he made the 50 kilims titled *Alternando da uno a cento e viceversa* [Alternating One to One Hundred and Vice-Versa], exhibited for the first time at the Centre National d' Art Contemporain in Grenoble (fig.63). He came to Grenoble, as serene and jovial as ever. Using a large pair of steel scissors, he checked the wool pile on every kilim. Late in the spring of 1994 thieves entered his house and, since he was there, it became necessary to kill him. It must have taken at least a hundred of them to overpower the slight, ironic person of Mr Azam.

Enomoto san. Master calligrapher of Tokyo, 1985.

Boetti sat himself down on the tatami mat. He had with him a package of large sheets of rice paper. He folded these sheets in different ways, then asked the calligrapher to draw a few ideograms: wind, order and disorder, folding and unfolding, Alighiero and Boetti. Enomoto san overcame his initial perplexity. When the ink was dry, Boetti unfolded the sheets of rice paper. The ideograms were no longer whole, nor were they broken. Only, the folds had formed white intervals in the continuity of the movement. Alighiero and Enomoto san were amused by this, satisfied.

Guido Fuga, Venetian illustrator.

I shall recall one thing alone, just for those familiar with Corto Maltese, a gentleman of fortune and a character in Hugo Pratt's comic strips. In the illustrated novel titled *Corte Sconta detta Arcana* (the name of a little square in the Old Ghetto in Venice, entrance into which requires that seven doors be opened), Fuga's drawings were the finest ever made of the armoured trains that ran on the Siberian Railway between 1919 and 1921, the most exquisite military fittings, and gun turrets, and braking mechanisms, and nuts and bolts. It was Guido Fuga who drew Boetti's *Aerei* [Aeroplanes], 1977 (fig.51).

Master Berang Ramazan, known as "the colourless". Peshawar. During the Soviet occupation of Afghanistan.

All these years later, I cannot be certain that I actually did come across the conspicuous sign board of his school of poetry, one warm afternoon in late January. I can remember a silent widening road behind the bazaar of jewels, not far from Chewk Jadgar. I can remember a whitewashed gravestone and the little multi-coloured flags with which it was bedecked. I can remember a canal and an alleyway, on the right, and a rectangular tea house: against the darkness of its far wall there was the chirping of an aviary. I later found the gravestone, the canal, other tea houses, one with a flooring of fresh straw and slender sky-blue pillars, but not the alleyway with the aviary and Sufi Berang's sign board. It is no cause for amazement in this city if things sometimes do appear and sometimes do not. This was the Sufi who put together a collection of "epic and agnostic poems" titled *Naghma ye Bismil or The Wounded Song* and gave it to Alighiero so that " he could use it in his efforts to propagate the culture of the heroic Afghan nation, particularly today (1988) during this period of its history which is full of bloody resistance and Jihad" (fig.60). Something which Alighiero indeed did, setting these poems into the tapestries which he exhibited at *Magiciens de la Terre* in Paris, an exhibition that was much seen and much discussed.

Out of an incomplete list - incompleteness being the nature of lists, completeness their presumption - I have chosen only these five embodiments of the Other. Each one of these people took part directly and creatively in one of Boetti's works. In Boetti's praxis, the Other is always a single individual, even if at times, behind this singularity, the Other is instantly collective, as occurred with the making of the tapestries, or the carpets, or the ball-point pens...500 Afghan women-embroiders, 100 inhabitants of Gavirate - a town in Lombardy - or the students of 50 French art schools....

At other times the Other is not a flesh and blood human being. We need to make a list here too, to justify this assertion. And here too I will offer just one example, in this case described by the artist himself in the statements made to a French magazine in 1992. The work in question was the one titled *12 forme dal giugno 1967* [12 Shapes from June 1967]. These are the maps which, over the course of those years, appeared on the front page of the Turin daily *La Stampa*: from the territories occupied by Israel during the Six-day War, up until the independence of Bangladesh from West Pakistan (fig.41).

" What interested me was that these drawings were not the fruit of my imagination, but of artillery bombardments, air raids and diplomatic negotiations".

fig.60
Poem by the Sufi Berang,
ca. 1988

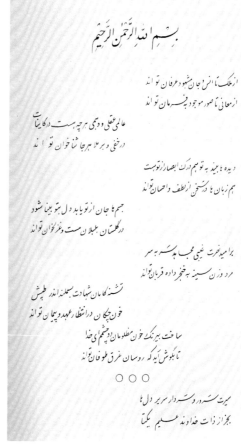

De bouche à oreille

This is one of the one hundred and fifty pairs of words which, we believe, Boetti placed in a square of sixteen letters, four by four, starting with "ordine e disordine" or else "order and disorder", and ending with this same French expression, which is very precise, very unequivocal. There is no translation in Italian; it would have to be "di bocca in bocca" [from mouth to mouth], which sounds like a news item going around, or like a succession of kisses. But De Bouche à Oreille (by word of mouth - literally from mouth to ear) retains a higher degree of objectivity, exactly because it is a concept raised to the power of two, therefore not an opinion, nor merely an idiomatic expression. It is a phrase which already exists in language and precisely in that self-same geometric form. It is a phrase which is much more something found, something discovered, than something invented. And besides, have we perhaps not said before, more or less explicitly, that Alighiero treats letters as though they were numbers and numbers as though they were letters, even if he does not express himself in either Sanskrit or Hebrew or Arabic?

Perhaps not. We have not yet said that Boetti, within a totally profane linguistic context, continuously attributed a numeric value to letters.

From mouth to ear means two things, as always in Alighiero's work, by which I mean at least two things and at any rate no less than two. The first of these is dialogue, the fact that every expression is realised, is made manifest always in the personal connection between one person and another. This is never a matter of solipsism, a subjective vision, even less so of an opinion, but always of a conversation between one person and another. This needs to be said in very practical, one might even say technical terms. From Mouth to Ear. With Alighiero, the word is not creative in itself, but only when it succeeds in being heard. Truth really only exists when it is received. It is in the act of exchange that truth asserts itself.

In a dialogue of this kind, the interlocutors need not be equal, nor even on the same level of consciousness. This is not a dispute between philosophers, but a dispute between different intelligences which only have intelligence itself in common. Sitting nearly always on a carpet, or else at a table, or at the telephone, Alighiero asks questions to which he has given a great deal of thought. For now his aim is to ascertain whether his is the only possible answer. Sometimes, the answer surprises the interlocutor himself, for he has not always understood the problem. What this means is to touch upon a secret. Dialogue is a technique for identifying secrets. If I keep a secret, it is not because I am loyal, but because I don't know that I am keeping it. From mouth to ear releases this very simple, very commonplace praxis, this necessity for there to be two people for a single truth to be understood.

Lastly, there is a second thing that Boetti means when he "squares" - amongst his last squarings - de bouche a oreille. With this phrase he affirms that the initial chain has not been broken.[4] Tradition is closely synonymous with transmission. The transmission of esoteric consciousnesses, from their original source - which, one should mention with extreme circumspection, is not human - has come about with neither mediation nor interruption, but by word of mouth: from Mouth to Ear. And such an affirmation from this joyous and somewhat sad artist, is very significant, his sixteen embroidered letters are very significant at this particular historical and spiritual juncture, known as *Kali Yuga*. It is a dazzling phrase set at the end of a dark time. During this time full of oblivion and pain, A and B had moved with infinite lightness, right from the day when a young man he knew all too well smiled at him from the window of a house which, at that very moment could not, by any means, have been lived in.

Giovan Battista Salerno

1 'To write with the left hand is to draw' – Boetti, who was not left-handed, wrote and drew these words with his left hand.

2 'Side' in Italian is 'lato', the Latin word from which the name of the Lazio region is derived. This region was Saturn's earthly hide-away. There is an expression which is still current in Italian: 'intendere il latino delle cose' [to grasp the Latin in things] which means to grasp their other meaning, or their hidden meaning.

3 In *Specchio cieco* [Blind Mirror], 1969, the artist appears at the mirror with his eyes closed, thereby respecting the symmetry of the specular image, but also accepting the fundamental splitting into two, in other words the Double, the doubling. This is precisely the way in which, after all, he derived the order of the alphabet when trying with difficulty to memorise it back to front; with the effort of someone who, not realistically wishing to subvert so vast a convention, nestles up alongside it, then doubles it.

4 'catena' [chain] translates the Hebrew *Schelscheleth* and the Arabic *Silsilah*, as well as the Sanskrit *parampara*.

fig.61
Boetti at the back of the 'One Hotel',
Kabul
ca. 1972

Shirazeh Houshiary in conversation with Mario Codognato

MC: When did you first meet Alighiero Boetti?

SH: I met him quite a few times, in Venice at the Biennales and again at the end of his life, during his exhibition in Grenoble, which was probably the last he was able to plan himself. I remember that it was already a very difficult time for him. He knew he was very ill and that he was probably going to die soon. We exchanged letters at the time, which included Sufi poems. He wrote a poem for me that described how a river would eventually join the ocean.

MC: Did you ever talk about his relationship to Sufism, in his work and also his life?

SH: Yes, we talked about these things many times. We often crossed each other's paths in our work. I think we belonged to the same tradition. He was one of the first artists who really made a constant effort to demonstrate that there is no opposition between East and West. I think that he saw both sides as complementing one another. Civilisation has developed from the union of these two cultures, and so did he. Nowadays everybody talks about this, but he was the first to state that there is no division in culture. Given that he was Italian, one could say that he belongs to the tradition of Marsilio Ficino, the Italian philosopher who translated Plato's dialogues into Latin. As early as the 15th century, Ficino posited that there is a precise link between East and West. He began with Zoroaster, then proceeded with Hermes, Orpheus, Pythagoras and finally Plato. He saw it as a chain, a link between Eastern and Western thought; almost as an umbilical cord. European culture does not develop out of nowhere. It goes back to the ancient Greeks, who go back to the ancient Egyptians, who in turn go back to the Babylonians. And to the Sumerians. People think that globalisation is a modern phenomenon, but this isn't the case, it has been happening for thousands of years. Boetti was fascinated by this cultural development, and I believe that, as a result, he became interested in Sufism.

Since the 18th century, but especially in our time, European culture has become reliant on matter. The modern philosopher or the modern thinker is always looking to science as a search for fixed knowledge. The Eastern tradition, on the other hand, sees everything in terms of rise and decay. So either you say that this world just developed through chaos or you follow the route that Plato, Pythagoras or the Sufis did.

fig.62
Senza titolo
[Untitled]
1988
embroidery
110 x 110 cm

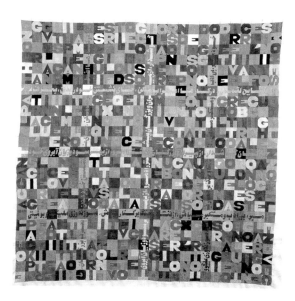

MC: A lot of people thought that Boetti was escaping from the West and that his attitude was a form of escapism. In fact, his interest in the links between East and West and in Sufism, as well as his numerous visits to Afghanistan, were actually a search for his roots, for his own links.

SH: Yes, it is absolutely important *not* to consider his work as a form of exoticism. There was no escapism. He was, on the contrary, looking for his and the West's roots, for truth, for the essentials. I think that anybody who wants to lead a creative life has to go back to these essentials. Boetti was one of the first artists this century to do so openly. Other people may have followed the same path, but if so in a rather veiled way, because they were afraid of being accused of all manner of strange things. Boetti was courageous enough not to be scared of this. He went to Afghanistan, worked there and perhaps discovered Sufism there. But Sufism is not something exotic. It has to do with the rational mind, if you like; reason operating in harmony with intuition. 'Harmony', incidentally, is a word invented by Pythagoras. Sufism is about making harmony out of chaos.

MC: Boetti's work also deals with the harmony of opposites and with the dualistic relationship between opposites. If I am not mistaken, that is something very close to the philosophy of Sufism.

SH: Yes, that's right. But as I said earlier, Sufism is part of a wider historical tradition. Both Plato and Pythagoras also believed that opposites have to come together. It is the unity of opposites that creates harmony in the universe.

Sufism is a tradition that is practised today. It's theories are alive, unlike those of Plato or Pythagoras, although in Western culture they have sadly been lost. Many people have struggled to keep it alive but slowly, because of the scientific approach, they have had to yield. They have lost a vision.

Truth is not so simple. It is not a question of either/or, but rather of two opposite things and, simultaneously, all things. It is a container of all, it's not something that can be separated. That's why I think Boetti had this fascination for Sufism, because with it he shared the belief that without the opposite there is no manifestation, no creation, no universe. It is through opposites that you reach the unity of the universe. Once you see its oneness, you see Truth as a whole; everything is encompassed within it.

MC: One of Boetti's last works was called *Tutto* [Everything]. Standing back it appears as a unified whole but, on closer inspection, one perceives that it consists of thousands of individual shapes (fig.56).
SH: This is very close to Sufism, as is his fascination with numbers and letters. Again, this is also connected to Pythagoras. Numbers can be seen as the essence of things, of reality, because they are abstract. Nothing in the world is more abstract than numbers are. For example, I can say 'one' to show you one thing, but I cannot show you the oneness. The idea of oneness only exists in the mind. Although numbers belong to the physical world, they are hidden, as though they were only a figment and not part of physical reality. Yet at the same time they are its essence.

Language also fascinated Boetti. What is language? It is the breath; in Genesis it is the word. It is the closest thing to our own force of life. The relationship between language and numbers is a return toward the essence. Many artists have worked with numbers, but by removing their meaning. Boetti, on the other hand, reinvested numbers with meaning.

MC: Within the number-letter relationship, Boetti was also fascinated by the shape of the square and how one could fit letters into it. Does this also come from Sufism and, previously, from ancient Greek thought?
SH: There were three traditions in ancient Greece: reason, the organic (which Aristotle adhered to) and magic. Plato, for example, belongs to the magical tradition, although he didn't necessarily negate rational or scientific thought. I believe Boetti also belongs to the magical tradition. He saw the possibility of containing the universe within the magical square and also saw the many different directions that possibility could take. These directions could be expressed through numbers (the essence), or through the alphabet (the word). In the beginning, according to the ancient Egyptian creation myth, the universe consisted of undifferentiated watery substances out of which came a cry. That cry was the word. Without the word there could be no form. Boetti played with this idea through the magical square, which he saw as an ideal form. The letters were like the essence of things.

Sadly, the magical tradition is not central to contemporary philosophy, but rather at the periphery. It has been replaced by a sort of artificial logic. This is why there is such a struggle. Around fifteen years ago a physicist stated that the universe is expanding and contracting. Now we have learnt that the universe is not contracting, but only expanding. This constant change is due to the fact that we rely on something one cannot even hold onto. No matter how much you break atoms down into smaller entities, you realise you know nothing, absolutely nothing. The beauty of belonging to the magical tradition is that you see the universe as a whole. When you see things as a whole, life changes, and there is a possibility of movement. The universe is created from movement alone; without movement there is no creation. It is beautiful that physicists are now coming to the same conclusions. Matter does not exist: electrons encircle a nucleus and their flow and movement result in the appearance of matter. So the universe is seen as one indivisible reality forever in motion. It is fascinating that the Western world has had to go through a scientific vision in order to reach the same conclusions.

MC: Is Boetti's understanding of time as a very subjective concept also related to Sufism?

SH: Yes, there is definitely a connection. An investigation into the meaning of time was crucial to his work. Time is an invention of the human mind. Does it exist or have any meaning? Does it seem to exist simply because we are born, we live, we die? This is linear thinking; in Sufism, on the other hand, there is no concept of time. Only the moment exists. A true Sufi would only understand the existence of love and nothing else. Physicists are constantly trying to answer the question of life and to explain our relationship with time. But there is no answer. If one existed they would have found it by now. Every time they think they have an answer it escapes them.

If you could reach this small, minute moment of now, it would contain all, from the beginning to the end of time. As if to say that it is the smallest part and yet the largest. Boetti reached the same conclusions; and even if a lifetime is not long enough to fully comprehend, I feel that he died too early. There was so much for him to do, but somehow maybe he saw it at the end of his life. I am also referring to the last things he wrote to me about the river that would join the ocean. The whole of humanity can be seen as a tiny drop that becomes one with the ocean. Perhaps he saw it as a whole. I feel that he did.

fig.63*
Alternando da uno a cento e viceversa
[Alternating One to One Hundred and Vice Versa]
1993
woven wool and cotton
300 x 300 cm ca.
Collection Agata Boetti, Paris

fig.64*
Senza titolo
[Untitled]
1994 ca.
wool
350 x 240 cm
Collection Agata Boetti, Paris
and Matteo Boetti, Rome

fig.65
Strumento musicale
[Musical Instrument]
1970
photographic print
dimensions variable

Sol LeWitt in conversation with Antonella Soldaini

AS: Between 1969 and 1970 you and Boetti took part in similar exhibitions, such as *When Attitudes Become Form* and *Conceptual art arte povera land art*. Did you meet him at the time?

SL: I first met Alighiero when, in 1970, I came to Italy to do a show at Gian Enzo Sperone Gallery, and to do a piece at the Galleria Civica in Turin as part of *Conceptual art arte povera land art*. Many of the artists from Turin were in this show. I got to know Alighiero, Mario and Marisa Merz, Giulio Paolini, Gilberto Zorio, Giovanni Anselmo and SALVO at that time.

AS: What connections do you think there were at the time between American and Italian artists?

SL: There was a lot of good feeling between all of us about the work we were doing. In fact, Alighiero let me stay in his holiday house in Liguria, at the Cinque Terre, as he was not there then. I didn't see very much of Alighiero because he had moved to Rome and when I was there we didn't meet. I was aware of his work during that period and liked it very much.

AS: After his first involvement with Arte Povera, Boetti distanced himself from this movement and his practice evolved in different ways. He started to make works that openly related to minimal and conceptual art. How did you perceive such a crucial moment of his career?

SL: His approach to conceptual art was fanciful and imaginative. I don't think he was very much into the ideas of Arte Povera, although he was grouped together with them. He wasn't interested in the basic materials, for example, as much as basic ideas, number series and word associations.

AS: Some critics have quoted your seminal essay, 'Paragraphs on Conceptual art', 1967, as an example of affinities between your and Boetti's ways of working. Boetti did rely on a team of assistants to make his work, and for a while he even shared the same assistant with you. Apart from the formal results, how similar or dissimilar were your and his ways of involving others in your projects?

SL: He also, by necessity, used assistants to help him make his work. This included weavers in Afghanistan and helpers in his studio, who enabled him to complete works that were technically difficult and too complex for him to make himself. We both tried to find talented, intelligent and committed people, who also became our friends. They were usually young artists.

AS: Critics have often focused on Boetti's involvement with mathematics; he was indeed clearly intrigued by combinatorial and serial composition. How would you define Boetti's attitude towards this scientific world? Was it mystic, obsessive, or was it just playful?

SL: I don't think Alighiero was very interested in the scientific aspects of his work, or that he was particularly mystic. But to characterise his work as playful would be to misjudge and underestimate it. Like many conceptual artists, he wanted to work with ideas that were not ponderous, banal and heavy-handed. Although his ideas were serious and important.

fig.66
Postcard sent to Boetti from Sol LeWitt
1987

AS: On a more personal level, when did your relationship with Boetti become closer?

SL: I became closer to Alighiero in the 80s, when I lived in Spoleto and visited him in Rome and Todi. We traded work and became good friends.

AS: During the 70s Boetti started to exhibit in New York. In 1974, he was included in 'Eight Contemporary Artists' at MOMA, where he showed a blue 'biro' work. Unfortunately there was not much critical response. His work was either disregarded or, in some instances, misunderstood. Why do you think that at the time, and today still, he received so little attention?

SL: I would hope that his work will become better known, especially in the United States, where art writers tend to be parochial and, if not interested in American art, swept away into German neo-romanticism. The work of Boetti is the antithesis of this: it is cool, reflective, humorous. But as time goes on, I think that many of the Italian artists, including Boetti, will be re-evaluated and better understood.

Technical notes on the works of Alighiero Boetti
by Diletta Borromeo

These 23 notes list, in chronological order, the development of the artist's principal techniques, particular installations or events held in the course of his career. Each note details some examples of individual techniques, dating from their first appearance, in conjunction with the different iconography or working methods adopted by the artist. The numbering of these notes refers to the following general index:

1. **Indian ink on paper with technical drawing**

2. **Mixed media, using industrial materials that refer to objects**

3. **Mixed media, using industrial materials with either embossed or engraved lettering**

4. **Stickers on paper with different sequential combinations**

5. **Photography: Polaroid photography, photographic prints on paper or postal work**

6. **Pencil on squared paper with drawing**

7. **Tracing on paper with carbon paper, from newsprint or by impression**

8. **Photocopies on photocopying paper**

9. **Typography, limited editions**

10. **Events and performances**

11. **Mixed media on paper, postal works**

12. **Embroidery on drawing with letters, phrases and texts**

13. **Embroidery on drawing of a planisphere**

14. **Ball-point pen on paper with words and phrases or drawn images**

15. **Mixed media on paper, drawn images and writing**

16. **Ink on squared paper, drawing derived from mathematical procedures**

17. **Embroidery on drawing derived from mathematical procedures**

18. **Pencil or ink on paper with topical themes**

19. **Mixed media, limited edition**

20. **Embroidery on 'pack' drawing**

21. **Mosaic tesserae on drawing derived from mathematical procedures or images and writing**

22. **Weaving on drawing derived from mathematical procedures or images and writing**

23. **Mixed media, open air installations**

fig.67
Senza titolo
[Untitled]
1965
Indian ink on paper
70 x 100 cm

fig.68
Mancorrente metri 2
[Hand Rail 2 Metres]
1966
varnished chromium-plated iron
80 x 200 x 40 cm

fig.69
Eternit 9
[Asbestos Lumber 9]
1967
asbestos lumber
80 x 70 cm diameter

fig.70
Dama
[Checkers]
1967
perforated wood
52 x 52 cm

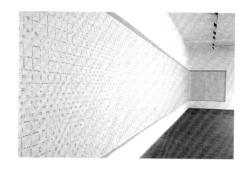

fig.71
Estate 1970
[Summer 1970]
1970
stickers and pencil on
lined paper
200 x 2,000 cm
Installation view at
Galerie Durand-Dessert,
Paris
1997.

fig.72
Bianco Saratoga 511 22 04
[Saratoga White 511 22 04]
ca. 1967
industrial varnish on
cardboard and cork
71 x 71 cm

fig.73
**Verso sud l'ultimo dei
paesi abitati è l'Arabia...**
[Southwards the Last
Inhabited Country is
Arabia…]
1968
plaster on board
185 x 159 x 6 cm

fig.74
Granbacino
[Largepelvis]
1968
Polaroid
2 elements: each 8.4 x 10 cm
used for folio n. 27 of the
publication *Insicuro
Noncurante* *
[Insecure Nonchalant]
1972-1975, edition of
41 + 4H.C. with Roman
numbering, 81 folios:
each 55 x 45cm

1. Indian ink on paper with technical drawing.

In 1965, the artist produced a series of works with Indian ink,
representing everyday objects (cups, glasses, bottles) and audio-
visual recording equipment (microphones, cine-cameras and
photographic cameras); these were drawn in the fullest detail with
the precision of technical drawings (fig. 67).

2. Mixed media, using industrial materials that refer to objects.

In 1966, Boetti began making assembla ges with materials that
referenced everyday objects. The materials include aluminium, PVC
plastic, asbestos lumber, cement, fire bricks (fig. 24), wood (fig. 21),
corrugated cardboard, printed fabric (see *Mimetico* [Camouflage],
fig. 35 and *Zig Zag*, fig. 28), sets of paper doilies made for cake shops
(fig. 4). Some of these works comprise accumulated components
made of the same material (fig. 69), while others consist of different
materials brought together and packed into a plexiglass container
(fig. 5). In the works titled *Dama* [Checkers] and executed in wood as
from 1967, the draught board layout of the components relates to
the tiny marks punched on each tile. The resulting series of
configurations only occur once within the work itself (fig. 70).

3. Mixed media, using industrial materials with either embossed or engraved lettering.

As from 1966, different techniques and industrial materials were
combined with either embossed lettering or engraved inscriptions.

The letters embossed on wood and cardboard panels form the title
of the work, which often matches the type of colour used (fig. 72).
The colour also sometimes alludes to the sound and/or meaning of
the phrase chosen by the artist (figs. 33 and 34).

On an iron cast made in 1970, the year of execution is spelt out in
relief, letter by letter. This panel is covered with green, spray-on paint,
which also spreads onto the wall. This procedure is repeated each
time the work is moved to a new location, thereby causing variations
in colour thickness (fig. 36).
Engraved lettering is also used on a plaster-cast titled *I vedenti* [The
Sighted], in which the artist made an inscription with the impression
of his own fingers. Other works that feature this form of lettering
use stucco or quick-setting cement marked, until possible, during
the progressive hardening of the material so as to produce a written
text (fig. 73 - the engraved text in this work is taken from
Herodotus, *The Histories*, 5th century B.C.).

4. Stickers on paper with different sequential combinations.

In 1967, using coloured stickers on paper, the artist applied a similar
working method to that adopted that year for *Dama* (fig. 70). The
stickers all vary in shape and colour, thus multiplying the number of
possible combinations. The artist developed variations on this
theme in *Estate 1970* [Summer 1970] (fig. 71), a large-scale work
whose title refers to the period of time entailed in its execution.

5. Photography: Polaroid photography, photographic prints on paper or postal work.

In 1968, Boetti had a photomontage made from two full-length
portraits, photographed at different times, in which the two
figures depicted are made to link hands. The resulting photograph,
titled *Gemelli* [Twins] (fig. 6), was printed in the form of a postcard
and sent out to friends and acquaintances over the course of the
year, with a variety of dedications. Recurrent among these are "

non marsalarti " [don't turn Marsala-sweet] and "de-cantiamoci su" [a pun on 'cantarci su': being carefree, or, 'decantare' which, in chemical terms, means to separate liquid from sediment].

During the same period Boetti experimented with Polaroid photography. In *Granbacino* [Largepelvis], the perspective of the feet leads us to imagine that the legs are parallel, while the rest of the body seems infinitely far away (fig. 74).

In 1975, on his return from Guatemala, Boetti printed five sets each of a series of four photographs, taken during the trip. Each photograph depicts the artist in the company of a local person, who had agreed to being photographed beside him. One of two prototypes of the pictures was given to the person involved (fig. 75).

fig.75
Guatemala
1974-1975
b/w photographic print
4 elements: each 26.5 x 19 cm ca.

6. Pencil on squared paper with drawing.

In 1969, Boetti produced a series of works with pencil on squared paper whose title derives from Antonio Vivaldi's opus 8, "Il cimento dell' armonia con l' invenzione" [The Contest Between Harmony and Invention]. On each folio the artist re-traced, free hand, all the outlines of the pre-existing squares, moving in different directions each time (fig. 13). In the example illustrated here (fig. 76), Boetti noted the following on completion of the work: "12 folios finished on 10 June 69, 43 hours". Sounds made during the making of these works were sometimes recorded. In some instances, the 12 folios that make up this work are arranged so as to be leafed through.

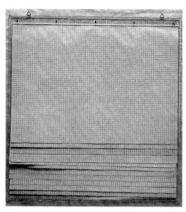

fig.76
Cimento dell'armonia e dell'invenzione
[Contest Between Harmony and Invention]
1969
pencil on squared paper
12 elements: overall
66.5 x 48.5 cm

7. Tracing on paper with carbon paper, from newsprint or by impression.

Tracing on different types of paper began with *Ritratto di Walter de Maria* [Portrait of Walter De Maria], in which a sheet of carbon paper was inserted between a photograph of De Maria and a piece of glass. By tracing the image this was transferred in thin blue lines onto the glass, which was then hung slightly apart from the wall (fig. 77).

Around 1973, tracing was obtained by superimposing a plain sheet of paper over the pages of daily newspapers: pressure applied to the outline of the newspaper images, showing through the plain sheet of paper, resulted in a partial transfer of the printing ink onto the plain paper. This procedure was also used for the first drawings of aeroplanes, to reproduce an iconographic form that, as from 1977, would become a recurring motif in works executed with a variety of techniques (see notes 14 and 15).

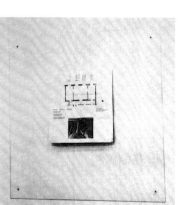

fig.77
Ritratto di Walter De Maria
[Portrait of Walter De Maria]
1969
tracing on printed paper, carbon paper and glass
ca. 60 x 50 cm

8. Photocopies on photocopying paper.

In these works, often titled *Autoritratto* [Self-portrait], the artist made photocopies of his face on paper, each time imitating a different letter of the silent alphabet. Placing its different folios side by side composes the title of the work. The work dedicated to Annemarie Sauzeau (fig. 79) bears the following inscription: "How to communicate with a machine which sees but does not feel. With the silent alphabet, used in bygone school days for mute communications. Annemarie has nine letters. There are nine Xeroxes". In an interview with Mariuccia Casadio, in the January 1991 issue of *Interview*, Boetti stated: "...I made another piece of work with two chicks...the Rank Xerox copier made a photograph of their little feet first of all, and these came out totally black. So you had something resembling a Chinese ideogram, formed by the three lines of the chick' s foot. Then there was the soft shadow of the body...But there were so many different ideas. I was saying that the photocopier is not just an office machine."

fig.78
Dossier Postale
[Postal Dossier]
1969-1970
typographic print, Rank Xerox paper and ink, edition of 99
181 elements: each 35 x 25 cm
Detail of ed. 12/99, bound in 3 volumes.

fig.79
Anne Marie
1969 (detail)
Rank Xerox paper
9 elements: each 33 x 21 cm

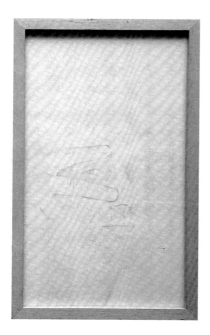

fig.80
Serie di merli disposti ad intervalli regolari lungo gli spalti di una muraglia
[A Row of Merlons Set at Regular Intervals Along the Ramparts of a Wall]
1971-1993 (detail)
mixed media on paper
13 elements: overall 25 x 350 cm

fig.81
720 lettere dall'Afghanistan
[720 letters from Afghanistan]
1973-1974 (detail)
Mixed media on paper, 720 stamped and franked envelopes
6 elements: each 165 x 120 cm, one book, 29.5 x 23 x 4 cm

fig.82
Giovedì ventiquattro settembre millenovecentosettanta
[Thursday Twentyfourth Semptember Nineteenseventy]
1970
simultaneous writing with two hands on wall
dimensions variable
Audio-visual recording made for *Identifications*, TV Exhibition II, curated by Gerry Schum
1970. Video-still transferred from b/w video tape, sound, 2.15 mins

9. Typography, limited editions.

Dossier postale [Postal Dossier] (fig. 78) was begun in 1969 and completed in 1970. 25 people were chosen, among other artists and friends of the artist, for the same number of 'journeys', to be enacted through the Italian postal service. Each journey consisted of a route leading through different geographical locations (with a total of 181 pre-determined stages).

Boetti sent a letter to one of these locations, with an address that did not correspond to the recipient's. The letter was therefore returned to the sender, who photocopied the envelope before placing it inside another one. The new envelope was then sent on to the next address for the same recipient, who yet again was un-reachable at that address. Each journey ended with the last envelope - containing all of the previous ones - returned to the sender, and with the photocopies of the envelopes themselves, documenting each individual stage of the itinerary. Occasionally the envelopes went astray, or the journey was interrupted for other reasons (the attempt to send an envelope to Ettore Spalletti on the island of Montecristo, for example, failed three times in a row because the island was not served by the postal service). The artist then decided to produce a limited edition of 99, using the photocopies and illustrating the routes followed on each of the 25 postal 'journeys'.

In 1972, Boetti began collaborating with Rinaldo Rossi's '2R' print works on the publication of *Insicuro Noncurante* [Insecure Nonchalant], a portfolio which - as displayed on the last card - contains "81 folios written by Alighiero Boetti between 1966 and 1975...". The edition consists of a selection of projects and studies, made with a variety of graphic techniques and some manual interventions, that relate to some of the works produced over that period. They were assembled over three years.

Among more recent editions, the book *Accanto al Pantheon* [Next Door to the Pantheon], 1991, was based on Boetti's joint project with the photographer Randi Malkin. The publication was divided into eight chapters, using Malkin's photographs to document eight days spent in the artist's studio at Via del Pantheon in Rome, between 20 January and 22 June 1989. Each day's topic was accompanied by a critical text.

10. Events and performances.

On 11 April 1970 Boetti took part in *Aktionsraum 1*, Munich. Participating artists had been invited (either individually or in pairs) to make an intervention using the audio-visual recording resources made available to them. Boetti presented a lecture and debate in Italian, preceded by a short introduction in Esperanto. The lecture was recorded. The artist also carried out a series of actions, including writing the words "Punto puntino zero goccia germe" (point dot zero drop seed) on the wall with both hands, to the right and left simultaneously. The words were taken from the translation, published in Italy in 1969, of Norman Brown's *Love's Body* (Random House, New York 1966). Boetti also substantially quoted from the book in the course of his lecture and the debate.

A publication documenting the *Aktionsraum 1* event as a whole, published in 1971, included images relating to Boetti's participation, together with a German translation of the texts.

In 1970, Boetti also recorded a performance for *Identifications*, TV Exhibition II, conceived by Gerry Schum. Other Italian artists who took part included Giovanni Anselmo, Pier Paolo Calzolari, Gino De Dominicis, Mario Merz and Gilberto Zorio. During the film, Boetti wrote on a wall in a similar manner to his performance at *Aktionsraum 1*, but this time the text read *Giovedì ventiquattro settembre millenovecentosettanta* [Thursday the twenty-fourth of

September nineteenhundredandseventy] (fig. 82). *Identifications* was presented at the Hanover Kunstverein on 20 November 1970 and broadcast by the Südwestfunk Baden-Baden on the 30th of that month, at 10.50 p.m.

11. Mixed media on paper, postal works.

The first of these dates from around 1970. On 4 May 1971, Boetti began a work he would only complete in 1993 (fig. 80). This consists of a series of telegrams the artist sent to himself, following a principle of exponential growth. The first telegram contains the words: "two days ago it was 2 May 1971"; on the second telegram, which was sent on 6 May 1971, the words are: "four days ago it was 2 May 1971"; on the third, sent on 10 May 1971, "eight days ago it was 2 May 1971". With this procedure, the time elapsed between each telegram progressively increase, until the last one - sent in 1993 – which reads "eightthousandonehundredandninetytwo days ago it was 2 May 1971". As the title metaphorically suggests, the telegrams were laid out horizontally one after the other.

In *720 lettere dall' Afghanistan* [720 letters from Afghanistan] (fig. 81) Boetti placed a sequence of 6 Afghan stamps - of different value and type – on each of the 720 envelopes. As with other postal works (fig. 46), the total number of envelopes depends on the quantity of possible permutations that can be derived from the initial sequence of stamps. In this case the envelopes, along with some folios that the artist had partly drawn on, were entrusted to his Afghan friend Dastaghir. The latter wrote some notes about his own daily life in the margin of the folios, then sent them from Afghanistan to Boetti's Italian address, using the envelopes that the artist had prepared. The letters were later collected in a book and exhibited together with the envelopes.

12. Embroidery on drawing with letters, words and texts.

In 1970, Boetti commissioned a section of square-meshed lace bearing it's date of production, spelt out letter by letter. The work adopts the same layout as that used for the cast-iron piece of the same period (fig. 83).

Subsequent embroideries were made on cloth and bore words, phrases or entire texts conceived by the artist. In most cases the letters are to be read from left to right and from the top down. These embroideries were produced by Afghan women, using traditional local colours but following certain rules laid down by Boetti. One such rule, applied especially during the 1970s, consisted in repeating the same combination of colours for those letters which appear more than once in the same work (fig. 84).

The text used in monochrome embroideries of 1978, contains the titles of some earlier works that had been executed with different techniques.

In 1970 Boetti and Annemarie Sauzeau had started working on *Classifying the Thousand Longest Rivers in the World*, published in 1977 (fig. 16). In 1976, as the project was nearing completion, the artist started planning an embroidered work that would list the names of the rivers, each numbered in decreasing order, starting with the longest, the Nile (fig. 87).

By the end of the 1970s, Boetti started to commission embroidered works which contained texts in Farsi, the language spoken in Afghanistan. Some ten years later, for *Magiciens de la terre*, held at the Pompidou Centre in Paris in 1989, Boetti presented an installation with 51 components, in which his texts alternated with the poems of the Sufi Berang (fig. 85).

fig.83
Millenovecentosettanta
[N-i-n-e-t-e-e-n-s-e-v-e-n-t-y]
1970
square-meshed lace
27 x 27 cm

fig.84
Nella vita errante fratello mio fisso abbi sempre l'occhio alla ciambella e mai al foro
[As You Wonder Through Life My Brother Always Keep Your Eye on the Doughnut and Never on the Hole]
1974
embroidery
39.5 x 39.5 cm

fig.85
Poesie con il Sufi Berang
[Poems with the Sufi Berang]
1988-1989 (detail)
embroidery
51 elements: each 110 x 110 cm

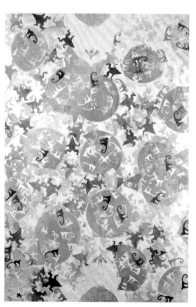

fig.86
La natura, una faccenda ottusa
[Nature, A Dumb Affair]
1981
mixed media on mounted paper
150 x 100 cm

fig.87
I mille fiumi più lunghi del mondo
[The Thousand Longest Rivers in the World]
1976-1982
embroidery
280 x 460 cm

fig.88
Mettere al mondo il mondo
[To Give Birth to the World]
1972-1973
blue ball-point pen on paper
2 elements: each 158 x 242 cm

fig.89
Mappa
[Map]
1984
embroidery
114 x 176 cm

13. Embroidery on drawing of a planisphere.

The embroidery of these works, called *Mappa* [Map], was begun between 1971 and 1972, and continued throughout the remainder of the artist's career. A drawing of a world map was marked out on a piece of cloth. Each territory was then embroidered with the colours and, where appropriate, symbols of its national flag, if the geographical area allowed room for it.

The colours of the seas and oceans vary (for example pink [fig. 43], dark red or black), but in most works these are blue or azure. Starting with the very first *Mappa,* most have an embroidered border. This encloses the image of the planisphere and contains a text by the artist, which is frequently accompanied by phrases in Farsi (figs. 44 and 89).

As time went by, the colours and symbols of flags were updated, taking account of historical events. One of the most recent works, embroidered by Afghan craftswomen during the break-up of the Soviet Union, was returned to Italy in 1992. The artist completed the work with some flags of the new republics (fig. 42).

14. Ball-point pen on paper with words and phrases or drawn images.

From 1972 onwards, Boetti developed works executed in ball-point pen, in the four standard colours (blue, black, red and green) and containing words or phrases. Three types of iconography can be identified in these works. In the first of these, the title of the work may be read by following the progressively arranged commas in relation to the letters of the alphabet, set out horizontally along the top margin of each panel (fig. 88).

In the second variant the alphabet is laid out vertically, often only on the first panel, so as to form an index that is referenced in reading subsequent panels (fig. 40). In the third variant, the use of a codified system of writing is abandoned and the title of the work appears across the top (fig. 90). Sometimes the text used corresponds to the artist's name rearranged in different ways, for example by grouping consonants and vowels together or by arranging letters in alphabetical order.

Works executed as from 1977 also include images, as in *Aerei* [Aeroplanes] (see note 7 for the first images of aeroplanes) or later *Pier Piet.* This last is a series executed in the four standard colours, and features the outline of a broken mirror, one of the many objects used by Boetti in numerous works on paper. Within this outline, a geometric protrusion hints at the shape of a pier, also indicated in the work's title.

15. Mixed media on paper, drawn images and writing.

In the early seventies, the artist began using a great variety of techniques on paper in different combinations. In the context of a wide-ranging output that continued into the nineties, it is possible to identify a substantial presence of images and hand-written texts that were executed with the left-hand. Over the years, the hand-written texts frequently appear in combination with figurative representations (fig. 32).

The first works in the *Aerei* series (fig. 51) were produced in 1977, in pencil and watercolour, as a collaboration with the illustrator Guido Fuga. Photographic paper, on which the images were reproduced, was sometimes used instead.

La natura, una faccenda ottusa [Nature, A Dumb Affair] (fig. 86), is a series of works produced as from 1980 in which animals appear as a recurring motif. The title is a reference to a phrase by Alfred North Whitehead (1861-1947), the English philosopher and mathematician, already quoted by Boetti in *Aktionsraum 1*. As from 1977, Boetti used a drawing based on the photograph *Due mani, una matita* [Two Hands, A Pencil] as a recurring image, always repeated twice and lined up to form a vertical axis (fig. 59). In 1987 the drawing also featured in the series of works titled *Tra sè e sè* [Between One and One's Self]. Within it, set along the vertical axis, are outlines of objects and forms in which colour and writing alternate (fig. 91).

16. Ink on squared paper, drawing derived from mathematical procedures.

Ink drawings made by filling in squares on squared paper were first produced around 1974 and replicate different mathematical schemas. In *Storia naturale della moltiplicazione* [Natural History of Multiplication] (fig. 92) the artist drew differing numbers of shapes, each made up of the same number of blackened squares (for example the first element in this work has nine shapes, each made up of nine squares). When the number of shapes is multiplied the number of squares is likewise multiplied, until the surface of the last folio is almost entirely covered in ink.

17. Embroidery on drawing derived from mathematical procedures.

In some embroidery works of the seventies and eighties, the letters spell out numbers which, together with mathematical symbols, form numerous variations on a single procedure. Once calculated, the result of this procedure in a single work is always the same number. In *Addizione* [Adding Up], for example, the result of the procedure is 1984 (fig. 48).

The procedure called *Alternando da uno a cento e viceversa* [Alternating One to One Hundred and Vice Versa], adopted in the embroidery works (fig. 93) - but which also featured in works on paper, mosaics or woven works (fig. 63) - is based on the alternation of one hundred black and white squares inside a grid of one hundred bigger squares. For example, the first big square contains ninety-nine smaller black squares and one white square, the second contains 98 white squares and two black squares, and so on. The last square, always a monochrome, is either black or white depending on which colour started off the process. The result of this process in each work is always a drawing containing 5000 white squares and 5000 black squares. The mechanism of alternating in this way can be respected while creating different shapes, since the layout of the filled in squares is not fixed.

18. Pencil and ink on paper with topical themes.

These works on paper are based on images of particular topical themes, taken from daily newspapers and from magazines, previously worked on in different techniques, and now painstakingly copied in pencil or in ink.

Two large-format folios were devoted to the subject of Gary Gilmore (fig. 18), the condemned murderer who refused to live on death row and asked, in 1977, for his sentence to be carried out. The first of these folios includes drawings of newspaper photographs alongside a text, quoted by Boetti, which gives an account of the execution. The second folio depicts various bodies lying on the ground (fig. 94).

In 1983 the artist began a series of works depicting the covers of periodicals published over a particular month or year (fig. 58), reproduced in pencil and sometimes with colour inserts. In 1990 he produced a work for Gianni Versace, featuring covers devoted to his fashion label.

fig.90
Mimetismo
[Camouflage]
1979
blue ball-point pen on paper
70 x 100 cm

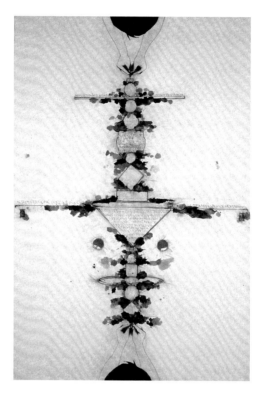

fig.91
Tra sè e sè
[Between One and One's Self]
1987
mixed media on mounted paper
150 x 100 cm

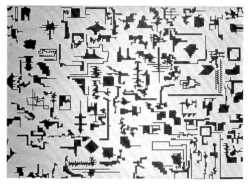

fig.92
Storia naturale della moltiplicazione
[Natural History of Multiplication]
1975 (detail)
ink on mounted squared paper
12 elements: each 70 x 100 cm

fig.93
Alternando da uno a cento e viceversa
[Alternating One to One Hundred and Vice Versa]
1977
embroidery
127 x 131 cm

fig.94
Gary Gilmore
1977 (detail)
Indian ink on paper
2 elements: each 100 x 150 cm

fig.95
Passepartout
1990
mosaic
380 x 320 cm

19. Mixed media, limited edition.

In 1977, Boetti showed *Orologio annuale* [Yearly Watch] (fig. 15) at Marlborough Gallery in Rome. Its face displays four numbers that together correspond to the year in which the watch was made. The watch was produced every year as a limited edition, of varying size, up until 1994.

20. Embroidery on 'pack' drawing.

These embroideries, titled *Tutto* [Everything] (fig. 56), were produced from the early eighties onwards and are based on drawings of an enormous variety of figures, objects and, occasionally, words. These highly-coloured shapes are made to join up, distinguishable by their fine outlines, and fit together to the point where they completely cover the available surface. The type of drawing these embroideries derive from is also known as *Pack*, and was employed in numerous works on paper in mixed media (fig. 12).

21. Mosaic tesserae on drawing derived from mathematical procedures or with images and writing.

In 1984, for an exhibition at Northridge University in California, Boetti used a mosaic technique combined with a drawing produced following the procedure of *Alternando da uno a cento e viceversa*. *Passepartout* (fig. 95), made in 1990 for the floor of Galerie Amelio Brachot, Paris, is also a mosaic tessarae, on a design featuring the five architectural orders of the arch, linked together and bordered with an inscription by the artist.

22. Weaving on drawing derived from mathematical procedures or with images and writing.

For his solo show at Grenoble in 1993, Boetti created an installation of 50 kilims. Each one had a different design and was produced, using the structure of *Alternando da uno a cento e viceversa*, by students from 29 Ecoles des Beaux-Arts as well as by other individuals involved by the artist. The working process began with 50 folders bound in red fabric and containing 100 folios, each filled by alternating black and white squares. The 100 components of each folder were photocopied and arranged on large-scale sheets so as to create the pattern of a kilim, life-size and in its entirety. This was then woven by Afghan craftswoment in Pakistan (fig. 63). The folders, together with the large-scale preparatory cartoons, were also exhibited at Grenoble.

In early 1994, Boetti initiated a carpet-weaving project. The central design, on a red, blue or black background, was built around a vertical axis from which extended patterns and coloured shapes which allude to numerous elements found in Boetti's practice. A text in Farsi bordered the edge of the carpet (fig. 64).

23. Mixed media, open-air installations.

For *Promenades*, organised by the Centre d' Art Contemporain in Geneva, the artist created *Palla corda* (Ball Rope), a metal cast which was to be set up in the Parc Lullin. This project was a variation on the work of the same name, conceived in 1968.

Subsequently, at *Sonsbeek ' 93*, Boetti set up another open-air installation (fig. 17). A bronze cast, taken from a mould of the artist's body, was connected to electrical and hydraulic attachments. The figure's feet were set in the ground while its hand held a metal tube from which water gushed out; on contact with the heated surface of the sculpture, this was immediately converted into steam.

Note on the dating of works:

Where a single date appears next to the title of a work, it indicates the year in which the work was made (eg. 1973).

When the making of a work cannot be attributed to a single year, the following have been adopted:

ca. indicates that the work was made in the period that spans the year preceeding the date given to the year after the date given. For eg.: ca. 1973.

( ) indicates that the work was re-made at a later date. For eg.: 1973 (1980)

+ indicates that the work was modified by the artist at a later date. For eg.: 1973 + 1980

– indicates that the work was made in the period between the two dates given. For eg. 1973-1974

Illustrations marked with an asterisk indicate works in the exhibition.

Biography and Bibliography

Alighiero Boetti
Turin 1940 – Rome 1994

Main Solo Exhibitions

1967
Alighiero Boetti, Galleria Christian Stein, Turin, from 19 January
Alighiero Boetti, Galleria La Bertesca, Genoa, December

1968
Galleria Christian Stein, Turin, from 7 February
Galleria De Nieubourg, Milan, 23 April-12 May

1969
Una vetrata - Io che prendo il sole a Torino il 24-2-1969 - Ritratto di Walter De Maria, Galleria Sperone, Turin, from 19 April

1970
Cimento dell'armonia e dell'invenzione, Galleria Toselli, Milan, from 22 May
Alighiero Boetti. 1970, Galleria Sperone, Turin, from 22 May
MANIFESTO 1967, Galleria Toselli, Milan, from 1 October

1971
12 forme dal 10 giugno 1967, Galleria Sperone, Turin, from 3 July

1972
Franco Toselli c/o Alighiero Boetti, Galleria Toselli, Milan, from 15 February

1973
Il progressivo svanire della consuetudine, Galleria Marilena Bonomo, Bari, from 17 February
Alighiero Boetti, John Weber Gallery, New York, 10-28 March
ALIGHIERO BOETTI Mettere al mondo il mondo, Sperone Gian Enzo & Fischer Konrad, Rome, from 12 May
Alighiero Boetti, Galleria Toselli, Milan, from 7 June

1974
ALIGHIERO E BOETTI, Kunstmuseum Luzern, Luzern, 12 May-16 June
Alighiero E Boetti, Galerie Annemarie Verna, Zurich, from 11 October

1975
ALIGHIERO E BOETTI, John Weber Gallery, New York, 8 February-12 March
"Zwei", Galerie Area, Munich, from 16 May
ALIGHIERO BOETTI PER UNA STORIA NATURALE DELLA MOLTIPLICAZIONE, Galleria Gian Enzo Sperone, Rome, from 10 June

1976
In folio, Studio Marconi, Milan, March
quadrare diagonando alighiero e boetti, Galleria Massimo Minini (Banco), Brescia, 30 October-20 November

1977
ALIGHIERO E BOETTI, Galleria Marlborough, Rome, from 16 February
ALIGHIERO E BOETTI, Centre d'Art Contemporain, Geneva, 7 October-2 November
Alighiero Boetti in collaborazione Guido Fuga, disegnatore, Galleria Il Collezionista, Rome, from 29 November

1978
ALIGHIERO BOETTI, Kunsthalle Basel, Basel, 4 March-2 April
Galerie Paul Maenz, Cologne, May
Pas de deux, Galleria La Salita, Rome, 11 May
Il libro dei mille fiumi più lunghi del mondo, Galleria del Cortile, Rome, June-July

1978-1979
ALIGHIERO E BOETTI, Galleria Christian Stein, Turin, 14 December-January

1979
ALIGHIERO E BOETTI, Chiostro di Voltorre, Seminari di Gavirate, Gavirate, 5-31 May

1980
1980, Salvatore Ala Gallery, New York, from 23 February
ALIGHIERO E BOETTI, Akao Art Agency, Tokyo, 27 June-26 July

1980-1981
ALIGHIERO E BOETTI La natura, una faccenda ottusa, Galleria Massimo Minini (Banco), Brescia, 19 December-30 January

1981
ALIGHIERO E BOETTI 1965-1981, Galerie Chantal Crousel, Paris, 21 February-26 March
ALIGHIERO E BOETTI, Galerie Annemarie Verna, Zurich, from 10 November
ALIGHIERO E BOETTI, Galleria Franz Paludetto LP 220, Turin, from 10 December

1982
Clessidra cerniera viceversa - Pack, Franco Toselli, Milan, from 30 November

1983
molo-la jetée-pier, Galleria Pieroni, Rome, from 11 February
I mille fiumi più lunghi del mondo, Galleria Franz Paludetto/LP 220, Turin, from 16 March
INSTALLAZIONI: Carla Accardi. Alighiero Boetti, Padiglione d'Arte Contemporanea, Milan, 21 April-23 May

1984
Alighiero e Boetti. Oeuvres récentes, Galerie Eric Franck, Geneva, 23 September-3 November
ALIGHIERO E BOETTI, John Weber Gallery, New York, 1-22 December

1984-1985
Alighiero Boetti, Pinacoteca Comunale (Loggetta Lombardesca), Ravenna, 15 December-27 January

1985
ALIGHIERO E BOETTI, Incontri Internazionali d'Arte, Palazzo Taverna, Rome, from 22 May

1986-1987
ALIGHIERO E BOETTI. Insicuro Noncurante, Le Nouveau Musée, Villeurbanne, 7 February-20 April; Villa Arson, Nice, 30 April-30 June; Stedelijk Van Abbemuseum, Eindhoven, 30 November-11 January

1987
ALIGHIERO E BOETTI Tra sé e sé, Galleria Lucio Amelio, Naples, 27 February-20 April
ALIGHIERO E BOETTI, Galleria Christian Stein, Milan, from 25 March
ALIGHIERO E BOETTI, Galleria Alessandra Bonomo, Rome, 7 May-30 June

1987-1988
Alighiero E Boetti, John Weber Gallery, New York, 5 December-9 January

1988
ALIGHIERO E BOETTI, Galerie Susan Wyss, Zurich, 3-16 June

1989
ALIGHIERO E BOETTI CIELI AD ALTA QUOTA, Galleria Toselli, Milan, 8 June-29 July

1990
PASSEPARTOUT ALIGHIERO E BOETTI, Galerie Amelio Brachot Pièce Unique, Paris, from 4 April
XLIV Esposizione Internazionale d'Arte. La Biennale di Venezia, solo exhibition at the Italian Pavillion, Venice, June
ALIGHIERO BOETTI, Salvatore Ala Gallery, New York, 17 November-15 December

1991
ALIGHIERO E BOETTI, Edward Totah Gallery, London, 16 October-9 November

1992
Alighiero Boetti Mimmo Paladino - DIECI ARAZZI, Galleria Emilio Mazzoli, Modena, May

1992-1993
Synchronizitat als ein prinzip akausaler Zusammenhange ALIGHIERO E BOETTI 1965-1992, Bonner Kunstverein, Bonn, 28 September-22 November; Kunstverein Münster, Münster, 4 December-24 January 1993; Kunstmuseum Luzern, Luzern, 12 February-14 April

1993-1994
De bouche à oreille, Le Magasin, Centre National d'Art Contemporain, Grenoble, 4 December-27 March

1994-1995
Alighiero e Boetti Alternating 1 to 100 and vice versa, Museum of Contemporary Art, Los Angeles, 7 August-4 September; The Institute for Contemporary Art P.S.1 Museum, New York, 9 October-8 January

1995
ALIGHIERO E BOETTI, The thousand longest rivers in the world / RICHARD LONG, Somerset willow line, Peter Blum Gallery, New York, February

1995-1996
Worlds envisioned: Alighiero e Boetti Frédéric Bruly Bouabré, DIA Center for the Arts, New York, 6 October-25 June; American Center, Paris, 6 September-28 January

1996-1997
Alighiero Boetti 1965-1994, Galleria Civica d'Arte Moderna e Contemporanea, Turin, 9 May-1 September; Musée d'Art Moderne, Villeneuve d'Ascq, 28 September-12 January; Museum Moderner Kunst Stiftung Ludwig, Vienna, 31 January-31 March
Alighiero Boetti 1967, Galleria Christian Stein, Turin, 10 May-30 June
ALIGHIERO E BOETTI. L'opera ultima, Galleria Nazionale d'Arte Moderna, Rome, 16 December-27 April

1997
ALIGHIERO E BOETTI onze oeuvres de 1965 à 1990, Galerie Durand-Dessert, Paris, 31 May-27 July

1998
Alighiero Boetti. Mettere al mondo il mondo, Museum für Moderne Kunst - Jahrhunderthalle Hoecst, Frankfurt, 30 January-10 May

1999
ALIGHIERO BOETTI, Galleria Seno, Milan, from 18 February
Alighiero Boetti, Galerie Guy Bärtschi, Geneva, 8 April-29 May

Main Group Exhibitions

1967

Il Museo Sperimentale d'Arte Contemporanea, Galleria Civica d'arte Moderna, Turin, April-May

Arte povera e Im spazio, Galleria La Bertesca, Genoa, 27 September-20 October

1967-1968

Con temp l'azione, Galleria Stein, Galleria Sperone, Galleria il Punto, Turin, from 4 December; Galleria Flaviana, Lugano, from 17 February

1968

Arte Povera, Galleria de' Foscherari, Bologna, 24 February-15 March

Il percorso, Galleria Arco d'Alibert, Rome, 23 March-16 April

Il Teatro delle mostre, Galleria La Tartaruga, Rome, 6-31 May

Prospect '68, Stadtische Kunsthalle, Düsseldorf, 20-29 September

RA/3 Arte povera + azioni povere, Antichi Arsenali della Repubblica, Amalfi, 4-6 October

1969

Live in your head. When attitudes become form. Works-Concepts-Processes-Situations-Information, Kunsthalle, Bern, 22 March-27 April; Museum Haus Lange-Haus Esters, Krefeld, 9 May-15 June; ICA, London, 28 August-27 September

Konzeption/Conception, Städtischen Museum, Leverkusen, October

Prospect '69, Städtische Kunsthalle, Düsseldorf, 30 September-12 October

1970

Processi di pensiero visualizzati. Junge Italienische avantgarde, Kunstmuseum Luzern, Luzern, 31 May-5 July

conceptual art, arte povera, land art, Galleria Civica d'Arte Moderna, Turin, 12 June-July

Kunstverein Hannover, Hannover, presentation of *Identifications*, TV Exhibition n. II, curated by Gerry Schum, 20 November

1970-1971

Vitalità del negativo nell'arte italiana 1960-1970, Palazzo delle Esposizioni, Rome, November-January

1971

Arte Povera 13 Italienische Kunstler, Kunstverein, Munich, 26 May-27 June

7ème Biennale de Paris, Parc Floreal Bois de Vincennes, Paris, 24 September-1 November

1972

De Europa, John Weber Gallery, New York, 29 April-24 May

Documenta 5, Kassel, 30 June-8 October

XXXVI Esposizione Internazionale d'Arte, La Biennale di Venezia, Venice, from 11 June

1973

Eight italians, Galerie MTL - Art & Project, Brussels - Amsterdam, 20 January-11 March

La ricerca estetica dal '60 al '70, Palazzo delle Esposizioni, X Quadriennale, Rome, June

1973-1974

Contemporanea, Parcheggio di Villa Borghese, Rome, November-February

1974-1975

Eight Contemporary Artists, The Museum of Modern Art, New York, 9 October-5 January

1975

24h su 24h, Galleria L'Attico, Rome, January

1976

Prospect retrospect, Europe 1946-1976, Städtische Kunsthalle, Düsseldorf, October

1976-1977

ALIGHIERO BOETTI Collo rotto braccia lunghe. SANDRO CHIA Immobilità: varii affetti. FRANCESCO CLEMENTE Coppia di inganno. VETTOR PISANI Oriente Occidente, Framart Studio, Naples, 22 December-22 January

1977

Arte in Italia 1960-1977, Galleria Civica d'Arte Moderna, Turin, May

1977-1978

16 Italiaanse Kunstenaars, Boymans Van Beuningen Museum, Rotterdam, 9 December-15 January

1978

XXXIX Esposizione Internazionale d'Arte, La Biennale di Venezia, Venice, from June

1980

PIER + OCEAN, Construction in the Art of the seventies, Hayward Gallery, London, 8 May-22 June; Rijksmuseum Kroller Müller, Otterlo, 13 July-8 September

XL Esposizione Internazionale d'Arte, La Biennale di Venezia, Venice, from June

1981

Identité Italienne. L'art en Italie depuis 1959, Centre Georges Pompidou Musée National d'Art Moderne, Paris, 25 June-7 September

1982

Avanguardia Transavanguardia, Mura Aureliane, Rome, April-July

Documenta 7, Kassel, June

1983

Eine Kunst geschichte aus Turin 1965/1983, Kölnische Kunstverein, Cologne, 8 October-13 November

1984

Il modo italiano, California State University, Northridge, 23 January-24 February

Coerenza in coerenza. Dall'arte povera al 1984, Mole Antonelliana, Turin, 12 June-14 October

1984-1985

Ouverture / Arte Contemporanea, Castello di Rivoli, Rivoli, 14 December

1985

Del Arte Povera a 1985, Palacio de Cristal, Palacio de Velàzquez y Parque del Retiro, Madrid, 24 January-7 April

The Knot. Arte povera at P.S.1, P.S. 1, The Institute for Art and Urban Resources, New York, October-15 December

1986

XLII Esposizione Internazionale d'Arte, La Biennale di Venezia, Venice, from June

1986 -1987

Ouverture II / Sul Museo, Castello di Rivoli, Rivoli

1987

Italienische Zeichnungen 1945/1987, Frankfurter Kunstverein, Frankfurt, June

1988

Made to Measure, Kettle's Yard Gallery, Cambridge, 16 July-28 August

1989

Magiciens de la terre, Centre Georges Pompidou Musée National d'Art Moderne, La Grande Halle - La Villette, Paris, 18 May-14 August

1989-1990

L'art conceptuel, une perspective, Musée d'Art Moderne de la Ville de Paris, Paris, 22 November-18 February

1990

"Arte Povera." La collection du Musée National d'Art Moderne, Musée Cantini, Marseille, in collaboration with Centre Georges Pompidou, Paris, 16 October-2 December

1990-1991

Rome Anni Sessanta al di là della pittura, Palazzo delle Esposizioni, Rome, 20 December-15 February

1991

QUE L'ART SURVIENNE, Festival d'Art Contemporain, Vienne-Isère, 1 July-31 August

1992

A visage découvert, Fondation Cartier, Paris, June

La Collection Christian Stein. Un regard sur l'art italien, Le Nouveau Musée Villeurbanne, June-October

Arte Povera, Kodama Gallery, Osaka, 19 October-12 December

1993

Un'avventura internazionale. Torino e le arti 1950-1970, Castello di Rivoli, Rivoli, 5 February-25 April

Sonsbeek 93, Arnhem, 5 June-26 September

XLV Esposizione Internazionale d'Arte, La Biennale di Venezia, Venice, 14 June-10 October

1994

Of the Human condition: Hope and Despair at the End of the Century, Spiral Wacoal Art Center, Tokyo, 1-20 February

Mapping, Museum of Modern Art, New York, 6 October-20 December

1994-1995

The Italian Metamorphosis. 1943-1968, Solomon R. Guggenheim Museum, New York, 7 October-22 January; Kunstmuseum Wolfsburg, 22 April-13 August

1995

XLVI Esposizione Internazionale d'Arte, La Biennale di Venezia, Venice, from 10 June

1996

Jurassic technologies revenant, 10th Biennale of Sydney, Sydney, 27 July-22 September

1996-1997

Face à l'Histoire, Centre Georges Pompidou Musée National d'Art Moderne, Paris, 9 December-7 April

1997

Skulptur Projekte in Münster, Westfälisches Landesmuseum and the City of Munster, Münster, 22 June-28 September

1997-1998

Arte Povera. Arbeiten und Dokumente aus der Sammlung Goetz 1958 bis heute, Neues Museum Weserburg, Bremen, 22 June-7 September; Kunsthalle Nürnberg, Nürnberg, 2 October-7 December; Kölnischer Kunstverein, Cologne, 14 February-26 April; Museum Moderner Kunst Stiftung Ludwig, Vienna, 19 June-30 August; Kunsthalle Göteborg, Göteborg, 19 September-22 November

Arte Italiana 1945-1995. Il visibile e l'invisibile, Aichi Prefectural Museum of Art, Nagoya, 14 November-15 January; Museum of Contemporary Art, Tokyo, 1 February-22 March; Yonago City Museum of Art, Tottori, 23 April-26 May; Hiroshima City Museum of Contemporary Art, Hiroshima, 15 June-26 July; Taipei fine Arts Museum, 18 September-15 November

1998-1999

Unfinished History, Walker Art Center, Minneapolis, 18 October-10 January; Museum of Contemporary Art, Chicago, 28 January-4 April

1999

Ars Aevi 2000, Centar Skenderija, Sarajevo, 25 June-7 September

Selected Bibliography

Solo and group exhibition catalogues

1967

Eugenio Battisti, Germano Celant, Aldo Passoni (eds.) *Il Museo Sperimentale d'Arte Contemporanea*, Galleria Civica d'Arte Moderna, Turin, Fabbri Editori, Milan

Germano Celant, Henry Martin, Tommaso Trini, *Alighiero Boetti*, Galleria La Bertesca, Genoa

Germano Celant (ed.), *Arte Povera e Im-spazio*, Galleria La Bertesca, Genoa, edizioni La Bertesca - Masnata, Genoa

Daniela Palazzoli (ed.), *Con temp l'azione*, leaflet, Galleria Il Punto, Galleria Sperone, Galleria Stein, Turin

1968

Pietro Bonfiglioli (ed.), *Arte Povera. La povertà dell'arte*, in 'Quaderni dé Foscherari', Galleria dé Foscherari, Bologna. Texts by various authors.

Maurizio Calvesi (ed.), *Il teatro delle mostre*, Galleria La Tartaruga, Rome, Lerici editore, Rome

1969

Germano Celant, Marcello Rumma (eds.), *Arte Povera + azioni povere*, Antichi Arsenali della Repubblica, Amalfi, edizioni Rumma, Salerno. Texts by various authors.

Konrad Fischer, Rolf Wedewer (eds.), *Konzeption/Conception*, Stadtische Museum Leverkusen

Harald Szeeman (ed.), *Live in your head. When attitudes become form*, Kunsthalle Bern. Texts by Scott Burton, Grégoire Muller, Tommaso Trini.

1970

Jean-Christophe Ammann, Josephine Troller, Irma Incichen (eds.), *Processi di pensiero visualizzati - Junge italienische avantgarde,* Kunstmuseum Luzern

Achille Bonito Oliva (ed.), *Vitalità del negativo nell'arte italiana 1960-1970*, Palazzo delle Esposizioni, Rome, Centro Di/edizioni, Florence

Germano Celant (ed.), *conceptual art, arte povera, land art*, Galleria Civica d'Arte Moderna, Turin, Fabbri Editori, Milan

1971

Germano Celant (ed.), *Arte Povera. 13 italienische künstler*, Kunstverein München, Munich

Achille Bonito Oliva, *7a Biennale di Parigi*, Parc Floreal de Paris, Bois de Vincennes, Paris, Centro Di/edizioni, Florence

1972

Various authors, *XXXVI Esposizione Internazionale d'Arte*, La Biennale di Venezia, Venice

Various authors, *De Europa*, John Weber Gallery, New York

Harald Szeeman (ed.), *Documenta 5*, Kassel

1973

Achille Bonito Oliva (ed.), *Contemporanea*, Parcheggio di Villa Borghese, Rome, Centro Di/edizioni, Florence

Nello Ponente (ed.), *X Quadriennale di Roma. La ricerca estetica dal 1960 al 1970*, Palazzo delle Esposizioni, Rome, De Luca, Rome. Texts by various authors.

1974

Jean-Christophe Ammann (ed.) *ALIGHIERO E BOETTI*, Kunstmuseum Luzern

Jennifer Licht (ed.), *EIGHT CONTEMPORARY ARTISTS*, Museum of Modern Art, New York

1975

Bruno Corà (ed.), *"Zwei"*, Galleria Area, Munich

1977

Renato Barilli, Filiberto Menna, Antonio del Guercio, *1960–1977, Arte in Italia*, Galleria Civica d'Arte Moderna, Turin

Segni e disegni: Alighiero e Boetti 1976, Galleria Marlborough, Rome

1978

Jean-Christophe Ammann (ed.), *Alighiero Boetti*, Kunsthalle Basel. Texts by various authors.

Achille Bonito Oliva (ed.) *XXXVIII Esposizione Internazionale d'Arte*, La Biennale di Venezia, Venice

Giovan Battista Salerno, Anne-Marie Sauzeau, *Pas de deux*, leaflet, Galleria La Salita, Rome

1979

Tommaso Trini (ed.), *La festa dell'immaginario visivo. L'art ventura*, leaflet, Chiostro di Voltorre, Gavirate. Texts by Alighiero Boetti.

1980

Gerhard von Graevenitz (ed.), *Pier + Ocean*, Hayward Gallery, London, Arts Council of Great Britain, London

Luigi Carluccio (ed.), *La Biennale di Venezia. Arti visive '80*, La Biennale di Venezia, Venice, Electa, Milan

1981

Germano Celant (ed.), *Identité Italienne - l'art en Italie depuis 1959*, Centre Georges Pompidou, Paris, Centre Pompidou and Centro Di/edizioni, Florence

1982

Achille Bonito Oliva (ed.), *Avanguardia Transavanguardia*, Mura Aureliane, Rome, Electa, Milan,

Rudi Fuchs (ed.), *Documenta 7*, Kassel

1983

Alberto Boatto, Giovan Battista Salerno, *Alighiero e Boetti*, Padiglione d'Arte Contemporanea, Milan

Wulf Herzogenrath (ed.), *Eine Kunst geschichte aus Turin 1965/1983*, Kölnischer Kunstverein, Cologne, Daniele Piazza Editore,Turin. Texts by Germano Celant and Marlis Grüterich.

Michael Smith (ed.), *Il Modo Italiano*, vols. I & II, University of California, Los Angeles, Regione Piemonte, Turin. Texts by various authors.

1984

Alberto Boatto (ed.), *Alighiero e Boetti*, Pinacoteca Comunale (Loggetta Lombardesca), Ravenna, Essegi Editrice, Ravenna

Germano Celant (ed.), *Coerenza in coerenza. Dall'arte povera al 1984*, Mole Antonelliana, Turin, Mondadori, Milan

1985

Germano Celant (ed.), *The Knot. Arte Povera at P.S. 1*, P.S. 1, Institute for Art and Urban Resources, New York, Allemandi & C.,Turin and Institute for Art and Urban Resources, New York

Germano Celant (ed.), *Del Arte povera a 1985*, Palacio de Cristal, Palacio de Velázquez, Parque del Retiro, Madrid

Rudi Fuchs (ed.), *Ouverture / Arte Contemporanea*, Castello di Rivoli, Rivoli, Allemandi & Co., Turin

1986

Maurizio Calvesi (ed.), *XLII Esposizione Internazionale d'Arte*, La Biennale di Venezia, Milan. Texts by various authors.

Franz Kaiser (ed.), *Insicuro Noncurante*, includes 'Manuale di Conoscenza' by Giovan Battista Salerno, Le Nouveau Musée, Villeurbanne

1989

Cieli ad alta quota, Galleria Toselli, Milan

Jean Hubert Martin, *Magiciens de la terre*, Centre Georges Pompidou, Paris. Texts by various authors.

Suzanne Pagé (ed.), *L'art conceptuel, une perspective*, Musée d'Art Moderne de la Ville, Paris. Texts by various authors.

1990

Laura Cherubini, 'Le divergenze dell'arte', in Giovanni Carandente (ed.), *XLIV Esposizione Internazionale d'Arte*, La Biennale di Venezia, Venice, Fabbri Editori, Milan

1992

Achille Bonito Oliva, 'Arazzi del tempo nello spazio', in *Alighiero Boetti Mimmo Paladino. Dieci arazzi*, Galleria Emilio Mazzoli, Modena

Luigi Meneghelli (ed.), *Arte Povera*, Kodama Gallery, Osaka

Annelie Pohlen (ed.), *Alighiero e Boetti 1965-1991. Synchronizität als ein Prinzip akausaler Zusammenhänge*, Bonner Kunstverein, Bonn; Westfälisches Kunstverein Münster, Münster; Kunstmuseum Luzern, Luzern. Texts by various authors.

Catherine Francblin, *La collection Christian Stein. Un regard sur l'art italienne*, Le Nouveau Musée, Villeurbanne, Le Nouveau Musée/institut art édition, Villeurbanne

1993

Achille Bonito Oliva (ed.), *XLV Esposizione Internazionale d'Arte*, La Biennale di Venezia, Venice, Marsilio, Venice. Texts by various authors.

Jan Brand, Catelijne de Muynck, Valerie Smith (eds.), *Sonsbeek 93*, Arnhem, Snoeck-Ducaju & Zoon, Ghent

Germano Celant, Paolo Fossati, Ida Gianelli (eds.), *Un'avventura internazionale. Torino e le arti 1950-1970*, Castello di Rivoli Museo d'arte contemporanea, Rivoli, Edizioni Charta, Milan - Florence

Adelina von Fürstenberg (ed.), *De bouche à oreille*, Centre National d'Art Contemporain, Grenoble. Texts by Giovan Battista Salerno, Angela Vettese.

1994

Germano Celant (ed.), *The Italian Metamorphosis. 1943-1968*, Solomon R. Guggenheim Museum, New York, Milan

Fumjo Nanjo, Susan Sontag (eds.), *Of the Human Condition: Hope and Despair at the End of the Century*, Spiral Wacoal Art Center, Tokyo

Robert Storr (ed.), *Mapping*, Museum of Modern Art, New York

1995

Jean Clair (ed.), *XLVI Esposizione Internazionale d'Arte*, La Biennale di Venezia, Milan. Texts by various authors.

Lynne Cooke, André Magnin (eds.), *Worlds Envisioned: Alighiero e Boetti & Frédéric Bruly-Bouabré*, DIA Center for the Arts, New York. Texts by various authors.

1996

Jean-Christophe Ammann, Maria Teresa Roberto, Anne-Marie Sauzeau (eds.), *Alighiero Boetti 1965-1994*, Galleria Civica d'Arte Moderna e Contemporanea, Turin, Edizioni Gabriele Mazzotta, Milan. Texts by various authors.

Sandra Pinto (ed.), *Alighiero e Boetti. L'opera ultima*, Galleria Nazionale d'Arte Moderna, Rome, Allemandi &Co., Turin. Texts by Maristella Margozzi, Anna Mattirolo, Massimo Mininni.

Lynne Cooke, *Jurassic technologies revenant. 10th Biennale of Sydney*, Art Gallery of New South Wales, Artspace, Ivan Dougherry Gallery, Sydney

1997

Marc Bormand (ed.), *Face à l'Histoire*, Centre Georges Pompidou, Paris, Flammarion, Paris. Texts by various authors.

Klaus Bussmann, Kaspar Koenig, Florian Matzner (eds.), *Skulptur Projekte in Münster 1997*, Westfälisches Landesmuseum and City of Münster, Gerd Hatje, Ostfildern-Ruit

Various authors, *Arte Italiana 1945 – 1995. Il visibile e l'invisibile*, Aichi Prefectural Museum of Art, Nagoya; Museum of Contemporary Art, Tokyo; Yonako City Museum of Art, Tottori; Hiroshima City Museum of Contemporary Art, Hiroshima

1998

Christian Meyer-Stoll (ed.), *Arte Povera, Arbeiten und Dokumente aus der Sammlung Goetz 1958 bis heute*, Neues Museum Weserburg Bremen; Kunsthalle Nürnberg; Kölnischer Kunstverein, Cologne; Museum Moderne Kunst Stiftung Ludwig Wien, Vienna; Kunsthalle Göteborg; Sammlung Goetz München, Munich; Ingvild Goetz, München

Francesco Bonami (ed.), *Unfinished History*, Walker Art Center, Minneapolis

Rolf Lauter (ed.), *Alighiero Boetti. Mettere al mondo il mondo*, Museum für Moderne Kunst and Galerie Jahrhunderthalle Hoechst, Frankfurt am Main, Cantz, Ostfildern-Ruit

Periodicals: articles, reviews, interviews

1967

Germano Celant, 'Appunti per una guerriglia', *Flash Art*, n. 5, Rome, November - December

Germano Celant, 'Poor Art - Arte Povera', *Bit*, n. 5, Milan, November

Germano Celant, 'Nuove tecniche d'immagine. Arte Ricca e Arte Povera', *Casabella*, n. 319, Milan, October

Tommaso Trini, 'Arte Povera a Genova', *Domus*, n. 457, Milan, December

1968

Angelo Trimarco, 'Arte Povera ed azioni povere ad Amalfi', *Flash Art*, n. 9, Rome, November

Tommaso Trini, 'Le pietre di Boetti', *Domus*, n. 464, Milan, July

1969

Jean-Christophe Ammann, 'Live in your head, when attitudes become form', *Art International*, Lugano, March

Pierre Restany, 'Povertà dell'arte povera', *Il Corriere della Sera*, Milan, 15 June

Tommaso Trini, 'Trilogia del creator prodigo', *Domus*, n. 478, Milan, September

1971

Tommaso Trini, 'Di videotape in videotappa', *Domus*, n. 495, Milan, February

1972
Tommaso Trini, 'ABEEGHIIILOORTT', *Data*, n. 4, Milan, May
1973
Mirella Bandini, 'Torino 1960-73', *NAC*, n. 3, Rome, March
B. Boice, 'Alighiero Boetti', *Artforum*, New York, June
P. Stitelman, 'Alighiero e Boetti', *Arts Magazine*, New York, June
Lea Vergine, 'Arte Povera e Land Art', *NAC*, n. 10, Rome, October
1974
Max Kozloff, 'Traversing the field...eight contemporary artists at MOMA', *Artforum*, New York, December
Tommaso Trini, 'Alighiero Boetti: i primi mille fiumi più lunghi del mondo', *Data*, n. 11, Milan, Spring
1975
Maurizio Fagiolo dell'Arco, 'Boetti: il principio di non averne', *Il Messaggero*, Rome, 22 June
1976
Tommaso Trini, 'Alighiero e Boetti, insicuro noncurante perchè leonardesco', *Data*, n. 21, Milan, May
1977
Maurizio Fagiolo dell'Arco, 'In quell'artista c'è uno sciamano', *Il Messaggero*, Rome, 23 March
1978
Anne-Marie Sauzeau, 'Boetti ordine e disordine', *Domus*, n. 582, Milan, May
1979
Giovan Battista Salerno, 'Due artisti della comunicazione: cos'è (Warhol), come si cambia (Boetti)', *Il Manifesto*, Rome, 3 June
1980
Germano Celant, 'Une histoire de l'art contemporain en Italie', *Art Press*, n. 37, Paris, May
1981
Lisa Licitra Ponti, 'Una edizione Alighiero Boetti', *Domus*, n. 620, Milan, September
Giovan Battista Salerno, 'Una ruota libera e una no', *Acrobat Mime Parfait*, n. 1, Bologna
1982
Germano Celant, 'Documenta 7', *Kunstforum International*, nos. 7-8, Cologne, 9 October
Bruno Corà, 'Alighiero Boetti. Un disegno del pensiero che va, dialogo con Bruno Corà', *A.E.I.U.O.*, n. 6, Rome, December
1983
B. Boice, 'I fiumi - i moli - senza titolo 1982', *Artforum*, New York, June
Dennis Zacharopoulos, 'Arte Povera oggi', *Flash Art Italia*, n. 116, Milan, November
1984
Giovan Battista Salerno, 'Alighiero Boetti, sciamano e showman', *Il Manifesto*, Rome, 21 December
1985
Alan Jones, 'L'exposition du mois: the Knot Arte Povera at P.S.1 New York', *Galeries Magazine*, Paris
1986
Germano Celant, 'The red and the black', *Artforum*, New York, Summer
1987
Carolyn Christov-Bakargiev, 'Alighiero Boetti', *Flash Art Italia*, n. 140, Milan, Summer
Alain Cueff, 'Alighiero e Boetti: Le paradoxe et son double', *Parkett*, n. 12, Zurich
Ida Panicelli, 'Alighiero e Boetti', *Artforum*, New York, September
Giovan Battista Salerno, 'Boetti: quattro volte un bivio', *Flash Art International*, n. 140, Milan, Summer
1989
Mariuccia Casadio, 'Stravagare arte come viaggio. Alighiero e Boetti 1969-1989', *Vogue Italia*, n.473, Milan, November
1990
Nicolas Bourriaud, 'Alighiero Boetti', *Beaux-Arts*, n. 77, Paris, March

1991
Mariuccia Casadio, 'Concept Boetti', *Interview*, vol. XXI, n.1, New York, January
1992
Nicolas Bourriaud, 'Afghanistan', interview with Alighiero Boetti, *Documents*, n. 1, Paris, October
Angela Vettese, 'L'ordine e il disordine di Alighiero Boetti', *Il Sole 24 Ore*, Milan, 11 October
1993
Luk Lambrecht, 'Sonsbeek 93', *Flash Art International*, n. 172, Milan, October
Francesca Pasini, 'Opera d'arte fatta dai postini', *Il Secolo XIX*, Genoa, 28 December
1994
Alan Jones, 'Alighiero e Boetti', *Galeries Magazine*, n.58, Paris, February/March
Angela Vettese, 'Alternando da 1 a 100 e viceversa', *Domus*, n. 756, Milan, January
1995
Robert Farris-Thompson, 'Alighiero Boetti & Frédéric Bruly-Bouabré, DIA Center for the Arts', *Artforum*, New York, March
Barry Schwabsky, 'Imaginary itineraries: Alighiero Boetti's 'dossier postale', *The Print Collector's Newsletter*, n. 3, New York, July/August
1996
Jean-Christophe Ammann, 'Retrospektive Alighiero Boetti', *Kunst Bulletin*, n. 9, Frankfurt, September
Marie-Ange Brayer, 'CARTES ET TERRITOIRES', *Parachute*, n. 83, Geneva, July/September
Alessandra Mammì, 'Premiata ditta Alighiero & Boetti', *L'Espresso*, n.19, a. XLII, Milan, 10 May
1997
Paolo Vagheggi, '"Minimalia" dai francobolli all'astrattismo', *La Repubblica*, Rome, 21 July
Benjamin H.D. Buchloh, 'Sculpture Projects in Münster, *Artforum*, New York, September
1998
Philippe Régnier, 'L'art contemporain à portée du Main', *Le journal des Arts*, Turin, n.56, 13 March
Didi Bozzini, 'Alighiero Boetti, Gilberto Zorio: les chemins de la liberté', *Ligeia*, nos. 25/28, Paris, October 1998/June 1999

Books about the artist
1988
Sandro Lombardi (ed.), *Dall'oggi al domani*, Edizioni L'Obliquo, Brescia. With a text by Alighiero Boetti.
1990
Martina De Luca (ed.), *ALIGHIERO E BOETTI*, Edizioni Essegi, Ravenna. With a text by Giovan Battista Salerno.
1997
Anne Pontégnie, Marianne van Leeuw (eds.), *Origine et destination. Alighiero e Boetti Douglas Huebler*, Société des expositions du Palais des Beaux-Arts de Bruxelles, Brussels. Texts by various authors.

Texts and books by the artist
1967
Alighiero Boetti, typescript produced for the exhibition at Galleria Christian Stein, Turin. Reproduced in: Jean-Christophe Ammann, Maria Teresa Roberto, Anne-Marie Sauzeau, (eds.), *Alighiero Boetti 1965-1994*, exh. cat., Galleria Civica d'Arte Moderna e Contemporanea, Turin, Edizioni Gabriele Mazzotta, Milan, 1996. Texts by various authors.
1971
Alighiero Boetti, 'Besprechungsvortrag', *Aktionsraum 1*, Munich. Texts by various authors.
1977
Alighiero Boetti, Anne-Marie Sauzeau, *Classificazione dei mille fiumi più lunghi del mondo*, Ascoli Piceno
1991
Alighiero Boetti, Randi Malkin, *Accanto al Pantheon*, Prearo Editore, Milan. Texts by various authors.

Interventions/projects for periodicals and books
1970
Alighiero Boetti, 'Nineteen hundred and seventy', *Studio International*, n. 924, July/August
1972
Alighiero Boetti, 'ABEEGHIIILOORTT', *Flash Art*, Milan, n. 33/34, May
1979
Alighiero Boetti, 'Da mille a mille', *Domus*, Milan, n. 595, June
1983
Alighiero Boetti, 'Clessidra cerniera e viceversa', *Domus*, Milan, n. 637, March
1986
Alighiero Boetti, 'Project for Artforum', *Artforum*, New York, Summer
1990
Alighiero Boetti, 'Collaboration Alighiero e Boetti', *Parkett*, n. 24, Zurich. Texts by various authors.

General texts for reference
1968
Udo Kultermann, *Nuove dimensioni della scultura*, Feltrinelli, Milan
1969
Germano Celant, *Arte Povera*, Gabriele Mazzotta editore, Milan
1971
Achille Bonito Oliva, *Il Territorio magico. Comportamenti alternativi dell'arte*, Centro Di/edizioni, Florence
1973
Lucy R. Lippard, *Six years: the dematerialisation of the art object*, Praeger, New York
1974
Willem Sandberg (ed.), *'73-74' an annual of new art and artists,* Harry N. Abrams, New York
Herbert Read, *A concise history of modern painting*, Thames and Hudson, London
1975
Achille Bonito Oliva, *Europe/America, the different avant-gardes*, Deco Press, Milan
Germano Celant, *Precronistoria 1966-1969*, Centro Di/edizioni, Florence
Lea Vergine, *Dall'Informale alla Body Art*, Turin
1979
Renato Barilli, *Informale - Oggetto - Comportamento*, Feltrinelli, Milan
1983
M. Emanuel, S. Harris (eds.), *Contemporary Artists*, London. Texts by various authors.
1984
Achille Bonito Oliva, *Dialoghi d'artista. Incontri con l'arte contemporanea 1970 - 1984*, Electa, Milan
1985
Corrado Levi, *Una diversa tradizione*, Feltrinelli, Milan
1988
Germano Celant, *Arte dall'Italia*, Feltrinelli, Milan
1989
Gemano Celant, *Arte Povera*, Allemandi & Co., Turin
1997
Alberto Boatto, *Narciso infranto. L'autoritratto moderno da Goya a Warhol*, Edizioni Laterza, Rome - Bari
Hans Ulrich Obrist, Guy Tortosa, *Unbuilt Roads. 107 Unrealized Projects*, Gerd Hatje, Ostfildern – Ruit
1999
Carolyn Christov-Bakargiev, *Arte povera*, Phaidon Press Limited, London

Alighiero e Boetti

Whitechapel Art Gallery, London
15 September – 7 November 1999

alimus

Alimus is an award winner under the Arts &
Business Pairing Scheme for its support of this
exhibition. Arts & Business is funded by the Arts
Council of England and the Department for
Culture, Media and Sport

A●B
Arts & Business
PAIRING SCHEME

The Henry Moore Foundation
The Glass-House Trust

Lenders to the exhibition

Agata Boetti, Paris
Caterina Boetti, Rome
Giordano Boetti, Rome
Matteo Boetti, Rome
Archivio Alighiero Boetti, Rome
Chiara and Francesco Carraro, Padua
Roberto Casamonti, Florence
Celant Collection, Genoa
Giorgio Colombo, Milan
Louise and Eric Franck, London
Maria Angelica De Gaetano, Rome
Galleria 1000 Eventi, Milan
Paolo and Alida Giuli
Goetz Collection, Munich
Bruno van Lierde, Brussels
Achille and Ida Maramotti, Albinea
Museum für Moderne Kunst, Frankfurt am Main
Annemarie Sauzeau Boetti, Paris
Helmut Schmelzer, Nürnberg
Galleria Seno, Milan
Gian Enzo Sperone, New York
Monika Sprüth/Pasquale Leccese
Stedelijk Museum, Amsterdam
Christian Stein, Turin
N. Trentalance
Gino Viliani

And private collectors that wish to remain
anonymous

The Whitechapel would also like to thank the
following for their contribution towards the
exhibition

Marina Bassano, Clinio Castelli Trini, Roberto
Casamonti, Germano Celant, Giorgio Colombo,
Francesca D'Alessio, Maria Angelica De Gaetano,
Bruno Di Marino, Barone Giorgio Franchetti,
Corrado Levi, Ruben Levi, Carolin Lindig, Andrea
Marescalchi, Franz Paludetto, Pierluigi Pero,
Rinaldo Rossi, Giovan Battista Salerno, Alessandro
Seno, Nanni Strada

Photographic credits

Claudio Abate, Rome
Giorgio Benni, Rome
Pieter Boersma, Amsterdam
Archivio Alighiero Boetti, Rome
Paolo Bressano, Turin
Mimmo Capone, Rome
Enrico Cattaneo, Milan
Giorgio Colombo, Milan
Ivan Dalla Tana, New York
F. Duvernay, Villeneuve d'Ascq
Franz Fischer, Bonn
Roberto Goffi, Milan
J.C. Mazur, Paris
Giorgio Mussa, Turin
Paolo Mussat Sartor, Turin
Photothèque des collections du M.N.A.M./CCI,
Centre Georges Pompidou, Paris
Foto Saporetti, Milan
Axel Schneider, Frankfurt/M
Philipp Schönbron, Munich

Exhibition

Exhibition organised by the Whitechapel Art
Gallery in collaboration with the Archivio
Alighiero Boetti, Rome

Curated by Judith Nesbitt and Antonella Soldaini
Organised by Andrea Tarsia
Co-ordinated by Anthony Spira
Exhibition and catalogue research and
documentation supervised by Diletta Borromeo

Catalogue edited by Andrea Tarsia
Translations by Liz Heron (G.B. Salerno and
D. Borromeo) and Andrea Tarsia (A. Soldaini)
Designed by Kate Stephens
Printed by Pale Green Press, London

Alighiero e Boetti is published by the Whitechapel
Art Gallery, London

©The authors, Archivio Alighiero Boetti, Rome,
the photographers, The Trustees of the
Whitechapel Art Gallery, London, 1999

Whitechapel Art Gallery
80-82 Whitechapel High Street
London E1 7QX, England
Tel: 020 522 7888

Distributed in the UK by
Cornerhouse Publications
70 Oxford Street
Manchester M1 5NH
Tel: 0161 200 1503 Fax: 0161 200 1504

ISBN 0 85488 120 4